SMP 11-16

Book YE2
Draft edition

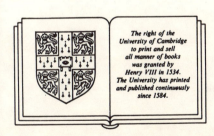

Cambridge University Press

Cambridge
New York   New Rochelle
Melbourne Sydney

Published by the Press Syndicate of the University of Cambridge
The Pitt Building, Trumpington Street, Cambridge CB2 1RP
32 East 57th Street, New York, NY 10022, USA
10 Stamford Road, Oakleigh, Melbourne 3166, Australia

© Cambridge University Press 1987

First Published 1987
Reprinted 1988

Diagrams and photosetting by Gecko Limited, Bicester, Oxon.
Photograph by Paul Scruton
Illustrations by David Parkins
Cover by Gecko Limited

Printed in Great Britain at the University Press, Cambridge

British Library cataloguing in publication data
SMP 11–16 yellow series.
Bk YE2
1. Mathematics – 1961–
I. School Mathematics Project
510   QA39.2
ISBN 0 521 31002 4

The authors and the publisher would like to thank the *Guardian*
for permission to use 'Alternatives' by Harford Thomas which
appeared in the *Guardian* on 3 April 1984.

Contents

1	Square roots	1
2	Coordinates with a difference	11
	Problems and investigations (1)	19
3	Areas, volumes, lengths	21
4	Quadratic functions	29
5	Random devices	42
	Problems and investigations (2)	48
6	Logic puzzles (1)	50
7	Polygons and polyhedra	51
	Problems and investigations (3)	60
8	Powers	64
	Problems and investigations (4)	78
9	Topics in solid geometry	80
10	Logic puzzles (2)	86
	Problems and investigations (5)	88
11	Simulation	89
12	The Fibonacci sequence	105
13	Rational and irrational numbers	112

Square roots

Some simple geometrical problems

1. A square has sides of length 10 units.
Find the length of a diagonal of the square.

2. A cube has edges of length 10 units.
Calculate the distance between a pair
of opposite vertices.

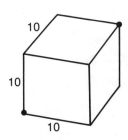

Question A1 is a straightforward application of Pythagoras' rule.
If d is the length of the diagonal, then
$$\begin{aligned} d^2 &= 10^2 + 10^2 \\ &= 200 \\ \text{So } d &= \sqrt{200}. \end{aligned}$$

At this point you probably reach for your calculator, and write down something like

$$d = 14 \cdot 14 \text{ (to 2 decimal places)}.$$

For most practical purposes this would be perfectly satisfactory, but $14 \cdot 14$ is only an approximation to $\sqrt{200}$.

3. Calculate $14 \cdot 14^2$.
By how much does it differ from 200?

The decimal for $\sqrt{200}$ goes for ever: $\sqrt{200} = 14 \cdot 142\,135\,6 \ldots$
No matter how many decimal places you take, you will still get only an approximation to $\sqrt{200}$. (If you calculate $14 \cdot 142\,135\,6^2$ on your calculator and get 200, that is only because the difference is too small to show on the calculator.)

1

In mathematics it is often important to leave an answer in the form $\sqrt{200}$, rather than replace it by a decimal approximation.

This is particularly true if you are going to use the value to work out something else. This applies, for example, in question A2.

You cannot work out the length AC straight away.
You need to work out AB first.

$AB^2 = 10^2 + 10^2 = 200$

So $AB = \sqrt{200}$.

Now use the triangle ABC.

$AC^2 = AB^2 + BC^2$
$= (\sqrt{200})^2 + 10^2$
$= 200 + 100 = 300$

So $AC = \sqrt{300}$.

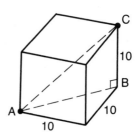

Notice that the answer here is written in the exact form, $\sqrt{300}$.
If you wanted a decimal approximation, you could always get one easily from a calculator.

In all the questions in this chapter, do **not** use a calculator.
Leave square roots in the form $\sqrt{200}$, $\sqrt{300}$, etc. (unless the number has an exact square root; for example, $\sqrt{25}$ can be replaced by 5).

A4 AB is of length 1 unit.
BC is at right-angles to AB and is of length 2 units.
CD is at right-angles to AC and is of length 4 units.
DE is at right-angles to AD and is of length 6 units.
EF is at right-angles to AE and is of length 8 units.

Find the length of AF.

A5 An equilateral triangle has sides of length 2 units.
Calculate its height.

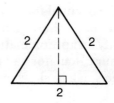

6 In this diagram, M is the midpoint of an edge of the cube.
Each edge of the cube is of length 6 units.

Calculate the length of AM.

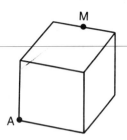

B Equivalent expressions involving square roots

1 (a) ABCD is a square of side 1 unit.

Find (remember: no decimals!)

(i) the length of the diagonal BD

(ii) the length of MB

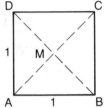

(b) Now work out MB in another way, as follows.

The angle AMB is a right-angle, and AM = MB. Let AM and MB both be x.

Use the fact that $AM^2 + MB^2 = AB^2$ to find x.

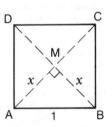

(c) Here is yet another way to work out x.

We notice that triangle AMB is a reduction of triangle BAD.

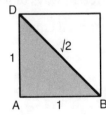   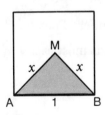

The scale factor of the reduction is the ratio $\dfrac{AB}{BD}$, which is $\dfrac{1}{\sqrt{2}}$.

Use this to find the length x.

Question B1 gives three different methods for working out the length of MB. The three methods lead to three apparently different answers.

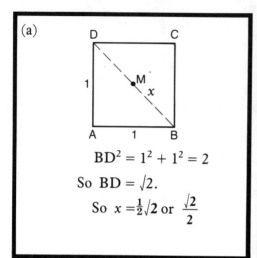

(a) $BD^2 = 1^2 + 1^2 = 2$

So $BD = \sqrt{2}$.

So $x = \frac{1}{2}\sqrt{2}$ or $\frac{\sqrt{2}}{2}$

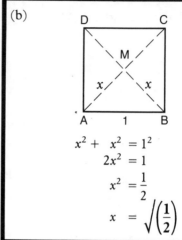

(b) $x^2 + x^2 = 1^2$

$2x^2 = 1$

$x^2 = \frac{1}{2}$

$x = \sqrt{\left(\frac{1}{2}\right)}$

(c) Reduction factor $= \dfrac{1}{\sqrt{2}}$

So $x = 1 \times \dfrac{1}{\sqrt{2}} = \dfrac{1}{\sqrt{2}}$

The expressions $\dfrac{\sqrt{2}}{2}$, $\sqrt{\left(\dfrac{1}{2}\right)}$ and $\dfrac{1}{\sqrt{2}}$ are all different ways of writing the same number. They look different, but they are all equal.

We can see this most easily by squaring them.

$\left(\dfrac{\sqrt{2}}{2}\right)^2 = \dfrac{\sqrt{2}}{2} \times \dfrac{\sqrt{2}}{2} = \dfrac{2}{4} = \dfrac{1}{2}$ $\left[\sqrt{\left(\dfrac{1}{2}\right)}\right]^2 = \dfrac{1}{2}$ $\left(\dfrac{1}{\sqrt{2}}\right)^2 = \dfrac{1}{\sqrt{2}} \times \dfrac{1}{\sqrt{2}} = \dfrac{1}{2}$

B2 Show by squaring that $\sqrt{\left(\dfrac{3}{4}\right)}$, $\dfrac{\sqrt{3}}{2}$ and $\dfrac{3}{2\sqrt{3}}$ are all equal.

$2\sqrt{3}$ means $2 \times \sqrt{3}$.

B3 Are $2\sqrt{3}$ and $3\sqrt{2}$ equal or not equal?

These five expressions look different, but some of them are equal to others. By squaring find out which are equal to which.

$$\sqrt{\left(\frac{3}{2}\right)}, \quad \frac{1}{2}\sqrt{6}, \quad \frac{\sqrt{3}}{\sqrt{2}}, \quad 3\sqrt{\left(\frac{1}{6}\right)}, \quad \frac{1}{2}(\sqrt{3} \times \sqrt{2})$$

Find out which of these expressions are equal to each other.

$$\frac{\sqrt{3}}{5}, \quad \frac{5}{\sqrt{3}}, \quad \sqrt{\left(\frac{9}{5}\right)}, \quad \frac{5\sqrt{3}}{3}, \quad \frac{3}{5\sqrt{3}}, \quad \sqrt{\left(\frac{3}{25}\right)}, \quad \sqrt{\left(\frac{5}{9}\right)}, \quad \frac{3}{\sqrt{5}}, \quad \frac{3\sqrt{3}}{\sqrt{15}}, \quad \frac{3\sqrt{5}}{5}, \quad \frac{5\sqrt{5}}{\sqrt{15}}$$

Earlier we found that $\frac{1}{\sqrt{2}}$ is equal to $\frac{\sqrt{2}}{2}$, and showed this by squaring.

Here is another way to show that they are equal.

$$\frac{1}{\sqrt{2}} = \frac{1}{\sqrt{2}} \times \frac{\sqrt{2}}{\sqrt{2}} = \frac{1 \times \sqrt{2}}{\sqrt{2} \times \sqrt{2}} = \frac{\sqrt{2}}{2}$$

This is just 1.

In effect, we have multiplied the 'top and bottom' of $\frac{1}{\sqrt{2}}$ by $\sqrt{2}$.
This is useful if we want to get rid of the square root on the bottom.

Here is another example. $\quad \dfrac{5}{\sqrt{3}} = \dfrac{5 \times \sqrt{3}}{\sqrt{3} \times \sqrt{3}} = \dfrac{5\sqrt{3}}{3}$

Some of these expressions are equal to others. Find out which are equal by getting rid of square roots in denominators.

$$\frac{3}{\sqrt{3}}, \quad \frac{6}{\sqrt{2}}, \quad \sqrt{3}, \quad 2\sqrt{3}, \quad 3\sqrt{2}, \quad \frac{6}{\sqrt{3}}$$

Three of these expressions are equal to each other. Which three?

$$\frac{2\sqrt{3}}{3}, \quad \frac{3\sqrt{2}}{\sqrt{3}}, \quad \frac{2}{\sqrt{3}}, \quad \frac{3\sqrt{3}}{2}, \quad \sqrt{6}, \quad \sqrt{3} - \frac{1}{\sqrt{3}}$$

This is a grid of 9 unit squares.

(a) Use triangle ABC to find AC.
(b) Use triangle APQ to find AQ.
(c) Deduce that $\sqrt{18} = 3\sqrt{2}$.

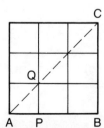

5

If we square $\sqrt{18}$ and $3\sqrt{2}$, then it is easy to see why they must be equal.

$(\sqrt{18})^2 = 18 \qquad (3\sqrt{2})^2 = 3\sqrt{2} \times 3\sqrt{2} = \underbrace{3 \times 3}_{9} \times \underbrace{\sqrt{2} \times \sqrt{2}}_{2}$
$\phantom{(\sqrt{18})^2 = 18 \qquad (3\sqrt{2})^2 = 3\sqrt{2} \times 3\sqrt{2}} = 18$

Note. This argument works only because we know that we are dealing here with **positive** numbers. Otherwise we **can't** deduce from the fact that a^2 is equal to b^2 that a must be equal to b.

For example, $(^-5)^2 = 5^2$ because both are equal to 25.
But it does not follow that $^-5$ is equal to 5.

The symbol $\sqrt{}$ means the **positive** square root, so this difficulty does not arise in this chapter.

B9 These ten different-looking numbers are in fact equal in pairs. Find out which pairs are equal by squaring.

$\sqrt{8} \quad 5\sqrt{2} \quad \sqrt{50} \quad \sqrt{96} \quad 10\sqrt{2} \quad 2\sqrt{2} \quad \sqrt{12} \quad 4\sqrt{6} \quad \sqrt{200} \quad 2\sqrt{3}$

C Products

If you multiply $\sqrt{2}$ by $\sqrt{3}$ you get $\sqrt{6}$.
This fact can be proved by squaring. All we need to do is to show that if we square $(\sqrt{2} \times \sqrt{3})$, we get 6.

$(\sqrt{2} \times \sqrt{3})^2 = (\sqrt{2} \times \sqrt{3}) \times (\sqrt{2} \times \sqrt{3}) = \underbrace{\sqrt{2} \times \sqrt{2}}_{2} \times \underbrace{\sqrt{3} \times \sqrt{3}}_{3} = 6$

It follows that $\sqrt{2} \times \sqrt{3}$ itself must be equal to the square root of 6.

There is nothing special about 2 and 3 here. The general rule is

$\sqrt{a} \times \sqrt{b} = \sqrt{(ab)}$.

C1 Show that this rule is true by squaring $(\sqrt{a} \times \sqrt{b})$.

C2 Without using a calculator, find the value of $\sqrt{20} \times \sqrt{45}$.

It is sometimes useful to factorise a number under a $\sqrt{}$ sign and to use the 'product rule' the other way round.
This is useful if an expression can then be simplified by cancelling.

For example, $\dfrac{\sqrt{18}}{\sqrt{6}} = \dfrac{\sqrt{(6 \times 3)}}{\sqrt{6}} = \dfrac{\sqrt{6} \times \sqrt{3}}{\sqrt{6}} = \sqrt{3}$.

3 Simplify these expressions by factorising and cancelling.

(a) $\dfrac{\sqrt{18}}{\sqrt{2}}$ (b) $\dfrac{\sqrt{10}}{\sqrt{6}}$ (c) $\dfrac{\sqrt{10} - \sqrt{8}}{\sqrt{2}}$ (d) $\dfrac{\sqrt{3}}{\sqrt{15} + \sqrt{6}}$ (e) $\dfrac{\sqrt{3}}{\sqrt{12} + \sqrt{27}}$

4 How many different numbers are there in this list?

$\dfrac{\sqrt{8}}{2\sqrt{2}} \qquad \dfrac{\sqrt{24}}{\sqrt{6}} - 1 \qquad \dfrac{\sqrt{50} - \sqrt{32}}{\sqrt{2}} \qquad \dfrac{\sqrt{6}}{\sqrt{24} - \sqrt{6}} \qquad \dfrac{\sqrt{108} - \sqrt{48}}{\sqrt{75} - \sqrt{27}}$

Factorising sometimes leads to a simplification of a single square root. For example,

$\sqrt{18} = \sqrt{(9 \times 2)} = \sqrt{9} \times \sqrt{2} = 3\sqrt{2}$

This works here because 18 has a factor 9, which is a square number.

5 Each of these square roots can be written in one of the forms $a\sqrt{2}$, $a\sqrt{3}$ or $a\sqrt{5}$. Write each one in one of these forms.

(a) $\sqrt{50}$ (b) $\sqrt{12}$ (c) $\sqrt{45}$ (d) $\sqrt{80}$ (e) $\sqrt{180}$ (f) $\sqrt{200}$ (g) $\sqrt{2000}$

6 Simplify these expressions.

(a) $\dfrac{\sqrt{8}}{2}$ (b) $\dfrac{\sqrt{50} - \sqrt{8}}{3}$ (c) $\dfrac{\sqrt{8} - \sqrt{3}}{\sqrt{32} - \sqrt{12}}$

(d) $\dfrac{\sqrt{12} + \sqrt{20}}{2}$ (e) $\dfrac{6}{\sqrt{45} - \sqrt{18}}$ (f) $\dfrac{\sqrt{10} + \sqrt{90}}{4}$

7 An approximate value for $\sqrt{10}$ is 3·16.
Use this to find an approximate value for

(a) $\sqrt{40}$ (b) $\sqrt{1000}$ (c) $\sqrt{160}$ (d) $\sqrt{2 \cdot 5}$

D Brackets

First, here are a couple of reminders about multiplying out brackets.

(1) The expression $(a + b)(c + d)$ can be multiplied out as in the table on the right.

	c	d
a	ac	ad
b	bc	bd

Alternatively, it can be done by pairing off each term in the first bracket with each term in the second bracket.

$$(a + b)(c + d) = ac + ad + bc + bd$$

(2) The rules of signs have to be obeyed. For example

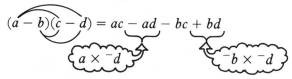

$$(a - b)(c - d) = ac - ad - bc + bd$$

($a \times {}^-d$)   (${}^-b \times {}^-d$)

(3) Squaring is a special case of multiplying out.

$$(a + b)^2 = (a + b)(a + b) = a^2 + ab + ba + b^2$$
$$= a^2 + 2ab + b^2$$

D1 (For practice.) Multiply out these expressions.

(a) $(x + 3)(y + 4)$ (b) $(x - 5)(y + 6)$ (c) $(x - 3)(x - 5)$

(d) $(2x + 1)(x - 4)$ (e) $(x - 3)^2$ (f) $(2x - 1)^2$

Here are two examples of multiplying out brackets which contain square roots.

$$(5 + \sqrt{2})(3 - \sqrt{7}) = 15 - 5\sqrt{7} + 3\sqrt{2} - \sqrt{14}$$

($\sqrt{2} \times \sqrt{7} = \sqrt{14}$)

$$(3 + \sqrt{5})^2 = (3 + \sqrt{5})(3 + \sqrt{5}) = 3^2 + 3\sqrt{5} + 3\sqrt{5} + (\sqrt{5})^2$$
$$= 9 + 6\sqrt{5} + 5 = 14 + 6\sqrt{5}$$

D2 Multiply out   (a) $(3 + \sqrt{2})(2 + \sqrt{3})$ (b) $(2 + \sqrt{3})^2$ (c) $(\sqrt{3} - 1)^2$

3 Multiply out these expressions.
   (a) $(\sqrt{5} - \sqrt{2})^2$ (b) $(3 + \sqrt{7})(3 - \sqrt{7})$ (c) $(\sqrt{3} - \sqrt{2})(\sqrt{3} + \sqrt{2})$

4 Multiply out $(\sqrt{3} + \sqrt{7})^2$. Use the result to decide whether $\sqrt{3} + \sqrt{7}$ is less than, equal to or greater than $\sqrt{(3 + 7)}$. Explain your reasons.

5 Simplify $(\sqrt{2} + \sqrt{18})^2$ in two ways:
   (a) by multiplying it out as it stands
   (b) by using $\sqrt{2} + \sqrt{18} = \sqrt{2}(1 + \sqrt{9})$

6 ABCD is a square of side 1 unit.

   The side AB is extended to E, so that AE = AC.

   (a) Explain why $BE = \sqrt{2} - 1$.
   (b) Use the right-angled triangle CBE to explain why $CE = \sqrt{(4 - 2\sqrt{2})}$.

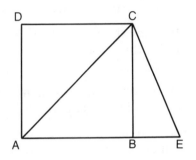

Further geometrical problems

1 ABCDEFGH is a cube whose edges are 10 units long.

   The four verticies A, C, F and H are the vertices of a regular tetrahedron.

   Calculate (no decimals!)

   (a) the surface area of the tetrahedron
   (b) the volume of the tetrahedron
   (c) the height of the tetrahedron if one of its faces is taken as the base

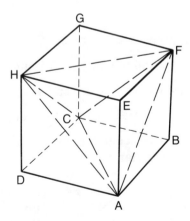

9

E2 Draw a square ABCD together with its diagonals. Let O be the centre of the square.

With centre A and radius AO, draw an arc to cut AB and AD at two points.

Draw similar arcs centred at B, C and D so that you have altogether eight points where these arcs cross the sides of the square.

Letter the eight points S, T, U, V, W, X, Y and Z, going round the square, starting with the point on AB which is nearer to A.

Draw the shape STUVWXYZ. What shape do you think it is?

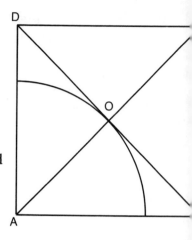

It is not difficult to explain why all the angles of the shape in question D2 are equal. (Make sure you can explain it!)

It is also easy to see that the sides ST, UV, WX and YZ are equal to each other, and that TU, VW, XY and ZS are equal. (Why?)

But it is not at all clear that ST and TU are equal.

To prove that they are, we need square roots. (Remember: no calculators.) The next question shows how to prove it.

E3 Suppose the square ABCD has sides of length 2 units.

(a) Find the lengths AT and BS.

(b) Hence find ST and TB.

(c) Find TU, and show that ST = TU.

(d) Deduce that the shape STUVWXYZ is a **regular** octagon.

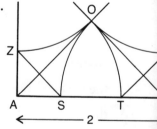

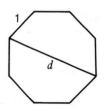

E4 The sides of a regular octagon are each of length 1 unit. If d is the diameter of the octagon, prove that

$$d = \sqrt{(4 + 2\sqrt{2})}.$$

Coordinates with a difference

Bipolar coordinates

A **locus** consists of all the points which satisfy a given description.

For example, the locus of all the points which are 1·5 cm from a fixed point A is a circle with centre A and radius 1·5 cm.

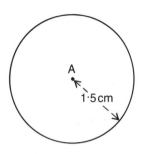

1 In the middle of a page, mark two points A and B, 10 cm apart.

Think of the locus of all points whose distances from A and B add up to 12 cm. Draw this locus in the following way.

> **1** Choose a distance from A, say 3·5 cm. The points which are 3·5 cm from A lie on a circle, centre A, radius 3·5 cm. Draw this circle.

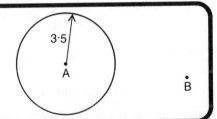

> **2** If a point on the locus is 3·5 cm from A, then it must be 8·5 cm from B, because the distances have to add up to 12 cm.
>
> Draw the circle with centre B and radius 8·5 cm. The points where the circles cross belong to the locus.

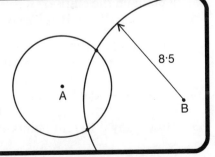

> **3** Plot more points on the locus in a similar way. Draw what you think the complete locus should look like.

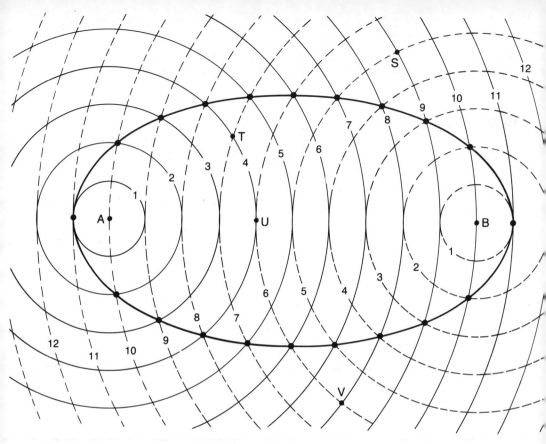

The locus in question A1 is in fact an ellipse.

Now think of any point in the plane of the paper (not necessarily a point on the ellipse). We can think of the point's distance from A and its distance from B as like two 'coordinates'.

For example, the point S in the diagram above is 9 units from A and 5 units from B. So its 'coordinates' are (9, 5).

A2 Write down the 'coordinates' of the points T, U and V in the diagram.

A3 How many different points are there with 'coordinates' (9, 5)?

We shall use r to stand for 'first coordinate' (distance from A) and s to stand for 'second coordinate' (distance from B).

We can write an equation for the ellipse. It is $r + s = 12$.

The coordinates *r* and *s* are called **bi-polar coordinates**.
(The points A and B are sometimes referred to as the two 'poles'.)

For the next questions you need worksheet YE2–1.

A4 Draw the locus of all the points for which $r + s = 15$, like this:

   (1) Mark as many points as you can for which $r + s = 15$. (As with ordinary graph paper, you can estimate values of *r* and *s* between those marked.)

   (2) Draw a curve through the points and label it $r + s = 15$. Remember that all the points on the locus must satisfy $r + s = 15$.

A5 Draw and label the loci whose equations are given below.

   (a) $r = s$ (b) $r - s = 3$ (c) $s = 1 \cdot 5r$ (d) $rs = 48$

A6 What inequality do *r* and *s* have to satisfy at every point of the plane?

A comparison

Ordinary (x, y) coordinates are called **cartesian coordinates** after their inventor, the French mathematician René Descartes (1596–1650).

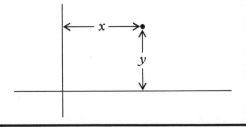

Cartesian coordinates can be thought of as the distances of a point from each of two fixed **lines** (at right-angles to each other).

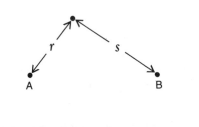

Bipolar coordinates are the distances of a point from each of two fixed **points**.

A7 (a) In cartesian coordinates, what loci do the equations $x = 1$, $x = 2$, $x = 3$, etc. and $y = 1$, $y = 2$, $y = 3$, etc. represent?

   (b) In bipolar coordinates, what loci do the equations $r = 1$, $r = 2$, $r = 3$, etc. and $s = 1$, $s = 2$, $s = 3$, etc. represent?

B Novel coordinate systems

In the cartesian coordinate system, we measure distances from two lines. In the bipolar system, we measure distances from two points.

We shall now investigate a system which is a kind of mixture of the two: distances are measured from one line and one point.

We shall use l to stand for the distance from the fixed line, and p for the distance from the fixed point.

We will write the coordinates in the order (l, p).

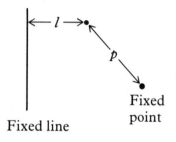

B1 Draw a fixed line, and a fixed point 5 cm from the line.
Sketch the locus of all points for which $l = p$.

For the next questions you need a sheet of special graph paper (worksheet YE2–2).
Notice that the graph paper shows negative values of l as well as positive values (just as in the cartesian system x and y can be negative).

B2 Draw the locus $l = p$. How good was your sketch?
The curve is called a **parabola**. Explain why the two ends never join up.

B3 Draw and label the following loci.

(a) $p = 0.8l$ (b) $p = 1.5l$ (c) $l + p = 8$ (d) $l + p = 5$

B4 What inequality is satisfied by l and p at every point of the plane?

B5 Make up some equations connecting l and p and investigate their loci.

In the coordinate systems we have looked at so far, the coordinates have been distances. It is also possible to have coordinates which are angles instead of distances.

We will now look at a system of this kind.

Let A and B be two fixed points. The line AB is drawn and extended beyond B to C.

Let P be any point in the plane of the paper.

The coordinates of P will be the angle PAC (denoted by θ) and the angle PBC (denoted by φ, pronounced 'fie').

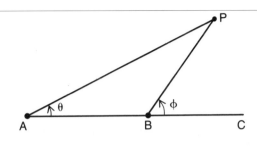

θ and φ are both measured **anticlockwise**. An angle of 20° below the line ABC can be thought of as either 340° or as ⁻20°.

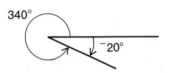

Graph paper for this coordinate system is on worksheet YE2–3.

B6 Draw the locus φ = 2θ.

Can you explain why the locus is what it is?

B7 Draw the locus φ − θ = 90°. Can you explain it?

B8 Draw the locus φ − θ = 60° and explain it.

B9 Draw the locus θ + φ = 60°.

10 Draw the locus 2θ + φ = 180°.

11 Investigate other equations and their loci.

We use a coordinate system to describe the positions of points on the Earth's surface.

The coordinates are called **latitude** and **longitude**.

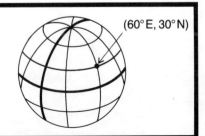

C Polar coordinates

We have looked at coordinate systems where both coordinates are distances, and a system where both are angles. In the system of **polar coordinates**, one coordinate is a distance and the other is an angle.

We start with a fixed point O, called the origin, and a fixed line, one end of which is at O.

Let P be any point in the plane.
The first coordinate of P is the distance OP, denoted by r.
The second coordinate is the angle between the fixed line and OP, measured anticlockwise. The angle is denoted by θ.

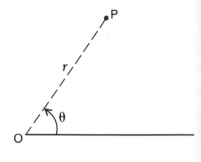

(r, θ) are called the **polar coordinates** of P.

Graph paper for the polar coordinate system is on worksheet YE2–4.

Polar coordinates are often used to show quantities which are functions of direction. For example the graph below shows the sensitivity of a microphone in a horizontal plane around the microphone. The distance r represents the sensitivity in each direction.

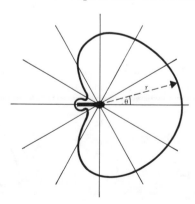

As with the other coordinate systems, an equation connecting r and θ corresponds to a locus. Before you plot points and draw a locus, it is a good idea to make a table of values of θ and r.

C1 (a) Copy and complete this table of values for the equation $r = \dfrac{\theta}{40}$.

θ	0	10	20	30	40	... and so on, up to 360
r	0	0·25	0·5	...		

(b) Draw the locus $r = \dfrac{\theta}{40}$.

Many interesting loci arise from equations involving trigonometrical functions of θ, such as $\sin\theta$, $\cos\theta$, $\sin 2\theta$, etc.

Often, when we substitute a value of θ into such an equation, we get a negative value for r. For example, if the equation is $r = 10\cos\theta$ and we let θ be $120°$, we get $r = {}^-5$. So we need to plot the point $({}^-5, 120°)$.

How should we do this? Think about it yourself, before looking up the answer on the next page.

C2 Make a table of values of θ and r for the equation $r = 10\cos\theta$. Do it for $\theta = 0°, 30°, 60°, 90°, \ldots$ up to $360°$.

Plot the locus on polar graph paper. What is it? Can you explain why?

C3 Do as in question C2 for the equation $r = 10\sin\theta$, and explain the result.

C4 The equations below produce some interesting loci, some with special names. Choose some of them and draw the loci on polar graph paper.

(a) $r = 5\cos\theta + 5$ (Cardioid)

(b) $r = 5\cos\theta + 2$ (Limaçon with a loop)

(c) $r = 5\cos\theta + 8$ (Limaçon with a dimple)

(d) $r = 10\sin 2\theta$ (Work out r for $\theta = 0°, 15°, 30°$, etc.)

(e) $r = 10\sin k\theta$ for other values of k.

D Investigation

So far we have looked at coordinate systems of the following types:

(distance from fixed point, distance from fixed point) *bipolar*

(distance from fixed line, distance from fixed line) *cartesian*

(distance from fixed line, distance from fixed point) ⎱ *in section B*
(angle, angle) ⎰

(distance from fixed point, angle) *polar coordinates*

Invent a coordinate system of your own and investigate some equations and their loci.

Negative values of *r* in polar coordinates

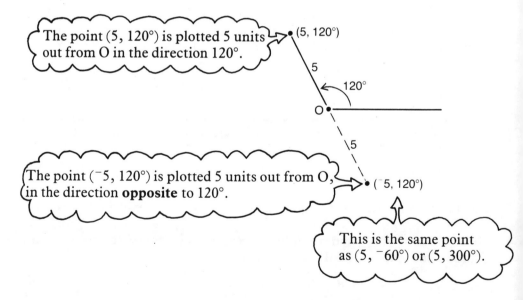

The point (5, 120°) is plotted 5 units out from O in the direction 120°.

The point (⁻5, 120°) is plotted 5 units out from O, in the direction **opposite** to 120°.

This is the same point as (5, ⁻60°) or (5, 300°).

Problems and investigations (1)

1. Jug A can hold 7 pints, but has only 3 pints of beer in it.

   Jug B can hold 4 pints, but has only 1 pint of beer in it.

   Jug C can hold 8 pints, but has only 6 pints of beer in it.

   How can you, by pouring from jug to jug alone, divide the 10 pints of beer into two equal parts?

   Can you find different ways of doing it?

2. (a) Can you replace the stars in this calculation by the digits 1, 2, 3, 4 and 5, each being used once and once only? If you can, find all the possible solutions. If it can't be done, explain why not.

   ```
      * *
    ×   *
    ─────
      * *
   ```

   (b) This time each of the digits 1, 2, 3, 4, 5, 6, 7 has to be used exactly once.

   ```
     * * *
    ×    *
    ──────
     * * *
   ```

3. This diagram shows a type of car jack. The four bars AB, BC, CD and DA form a rhombus. A is a fixed pivot on the ground. The point C is raised by turning the handle, which reduces the distance between B and D. P is the midpoint of AB and Q is the midpoint of BC.

   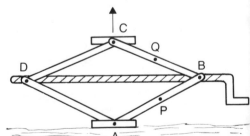

   The jack is slowly raised from its lowest position. Draw the path traced out by

   (a) P   (b) Q

   Can you explain why the path traced out by Q is what it is?

4 A single point is symmetrical about any line drawn through it. Every line through the point is a line, or **axis**, of reflection symmetry.

A single infinite line is symmetrical about any axis drawn at right-angles to it, and also about itself.

In what follows, 'line' will always mean 'infinite line', that is, one which extends indefinitely in both directions.

If we put a point and a line together, there is only **one** axis which is an axis of the point and an axis of the line, . . .

unless the point lies on the line, in which case there are **two** axes which are both axes of the point and axes of the line.

So a point and a line together can have two different kinds of reflection symmetry, this: and this:

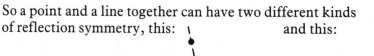
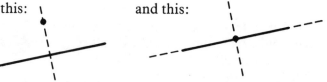

Find as many different kinds of reflection symmetry as you can for

(a) two lines   (b) two points and one line   (c) two lines and one point

(d) three points   (e) three lines   (f) two points and two lines   (g) four lines

Areas, volumes, lengths

A The area under a curve

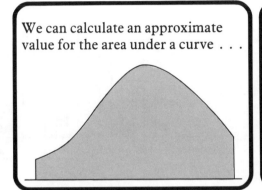

We can calculate an approximate value for the area under a curve . . .

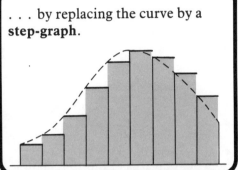

. . . by replacing the curve by a **step-graph**.

Let f be the function $x \to x^2 + 2$.

Here is part of the graph of $f(x)$ between $x = 1$ and $x = 4$.

We can get a crude approximation to the area under the graph by splitting the interval from 1 to 4 into six equal parts, each 0·5.

The heights of the rectangles in the diagram are $f(1), f(1·5), f(2)$, etc., up to $f(3·5)$.

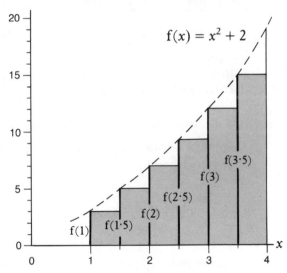

The total area of the six rectangles is

$$f(1) \times 0·5 + f(1·5) \times 0·5 + f(2) \times 0·5 + \ldots + f(3·5) \times 0·5$$

1 Using the fact that $f(x) = x^2 + 2$, calculate the total area of the rectangles.

We would expect to get a better approximation by splitting up the interval into steps of length 0·2.

The heights of the rectangles are now $f(1), f(1·2), f(1·4)$, etc., up to $f(3·8)$.

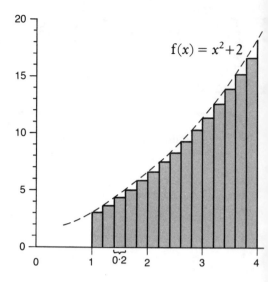

The total area of the 15 rectangles is

$f(1) \times 0·2 + f(1·2) \times 0·2 + f(1·4) \times 0·2 + \ldots + f(3·8) \times 0·2$

It can be easily be verified that this total comes to 25·52.

By splitting the interval from 1 to 4 into smaller and smaller steps, and doing a similar calculation each time, we can get better and better approximations to the area under the curve.

It is useful to have in mind a 'moving picture' of the area under a graph.

Think of x as **moving** from 1 to 4. The vertical line, whose height is $f(x)$, traces out or 'generates' the area.
As x goes from 1 to 4, the height $f(x)$ changes continuously as it traces out the area.

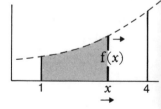

When we use a step-graph approximation, as in the calculation above, we make $f(x)$ hold its value for a while, then jump, then hold its value for a while, then jump, and so on.

This enables us to calculate an approximation for the area generated.

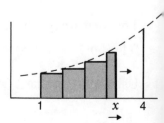

Note

If the starting value of f(x) is 0, then the first 'rectangle' under the graph will have area 0.

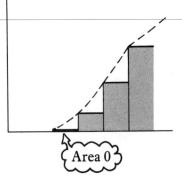

Area 0

3 Volumes

This diagram shows a gutter whose cross-section is the same throughout its length.

The cross-section is a semicircle of diameter 10 cm.

So the area of the cross-section $= \frac{1}{2}$ of πr^2
$= \frac{1}{2} \times \pi \times 5^2$
$= 39 \cdot 3 \text{ cm}^2$ (to 1 d.p.)

The gutter is 50 cm long, so its volume is $39 \cdot 3 \times 50 = \mathbf{1965 \text{ cm}^3}$.

You can think of the volume as being generated or traced out by the cross-sectional area A as it moves along the gutter.

Now suppose we have a gutter or channel whose cross-section is not the same throughout.

You can think of the volume as being traced out by the cross-sectional area as before. The difference is that the cross-sectional area is changing as it moves along the channel.

In the case of a real channel, such as a river, it would be impossible to measure its cross-sectional area at every point along it. But it is possible to make measurements of the cross-sectional area at intervals.

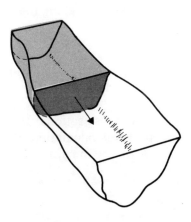

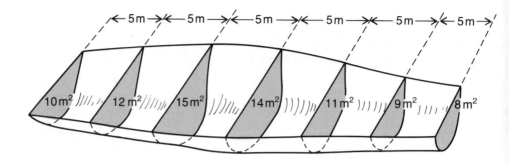

These area measurements have been made at 5-metre intervals along a channel. Suppose we want to calculate the volume of the channel.

We know the area changes continuously as we go along the channel, just as the height $f(x)$ changed continuously in the graph we looked at earlier.

In the case of the graph, we got an approximate value for the area by making the height $f(x)$ hold its value for a bit and then jump. So in the case of the channel, we can get an approximate value for the volume by making the cross-sectional area hold its value for a bit and then jump.

So we can calculate an approximate value for the volume like this:

(1) At the left-hand end, the cross-sectional area is $10 \, m^2$. Keep it at $10 \, m^2$ for the first 5 m along the channel. The volume generated is $10 \times 5 = 50 \, m^3$

(2) Now let the cross-sectional area jump to $12 \, m^2$. Keep it at $12 \, m^2$ for the next 5 m along the channel. The volume generated is $12 \times 5 = 60 \, m^3$.

(Total so far: $110 \, m^3$.)

B1 Complete the calculation above to find an approximate value for the volume of the channel.

B2 The cross-sectional area at the right-hand end ($8 \, m^2$) is not used in the previous calculation. But if we do the calculation from right to left we do use the $8 \, m^2$, but not the $10 \, m^2$ at the other end. Do it this way.

3 This drawing shows the cross-section area of the hull of a boat
   at intervals of 1 metre along the length of the hull.

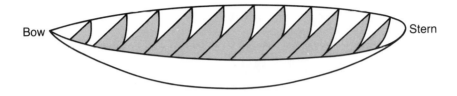

The actual measurements of the cross-sectional area are as follows.

Distance from bow, in m	0	1	2	3	4	5	6
Cross-sectional area, in m^2	0	0·7	2·5	4·1	5·3	5·8	6·1

Distance from bow, in m	7	8	9	10	11	12
Cross-sectional area, in m^2	5·7	4·4	3·6	2·4	1·3	0

Calculate an approximation for the volume of the hull. Notice that
the starting value of the cross-sectional area is 0 m^2, so keep the area at
0 m^2 for the first metre. Then jump to 0·7 m^2 for the next metre, and so on.

4 The diagram below shows an airship. The cross-section at every point
   along the airship is a circle. The diameter is given at 5-metre intervals
   along the length of the airship.
   Calculate an approximation for the volume of the airship.

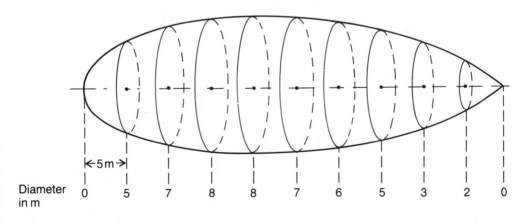

When you calculate an approximation to the area under a graph, you replace the graph by a step-graph, and the area by a set of rectangles. This area . . .   . . . is replaced by this

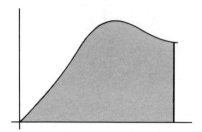
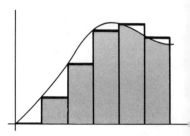

When you calculate an approximation to the volume of an airship, you replace the airship itself by a set of **cylinders**.

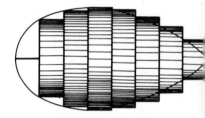

B5 Suppose the 'airship' is spherical, and of diameter 10 m.

(a) **Calculate** the radius of the cross-section at intervals of 1 m along the 'length' of the sphere.

(b) Calculate an approximation to the volume of the sphere.

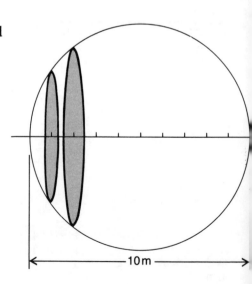

Lengths of curves

There are several practical methods for measuring the length of a curve. One method is to fit a piece of string or cotton to the curve, and then to stretch out the string and measure it.

Another method is to use a 'map measurer'. This has a little wheel on it which you roll along the curve. As the wheel turns it operates a pointer on a scale which tells you how far the wheel has moved.

Another method, which needs no special apparatus apart from a pencil and ruler, is the simple one of approximating the curve by a set of straight lines and measuring the total length of these lines. (The result will always be less than the true length.)

The points marked on the curve do not have to be equally spaced. One big advantage of this method is that we can improve on the accuracy by merely using more points, or better placed points.

The next question shows how this method can be used to approximate the length of a curve whose (x, y) equation is given.

1 This is the graph of $y = \dfrac{x^2}{5}$, for values of x from 0 to 5. The marked points are at $x = 0, 1, 2, 3, 4$ and 5.

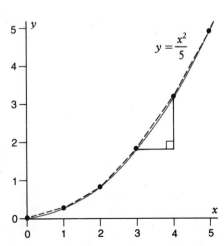

(a) Calculate the total length of the dotted lines. (The right-angled triangle is drawn as a hint.)

(b) Do the same calculation when the points are at $x = 0, 0{\cdot}5, 1, 1{\cdot}5$, etc. This gives a better approximation to the length of the curve.

C2 This curve is a quarter-circle of radius 5 cm.

(a) Calculate the y-coordinates of the points on the curve where x is 0, 1, 2, 3, 4 and 5.

(b) Calculate the total length of the dotted lines.

(c) Calculate a better approximation to the length of the curve by using points on the curve where x is 0·5, 1, 1·5, 2, etc.

(d) Compare this second approximation with the length as calculated using the value of π on your calculator.

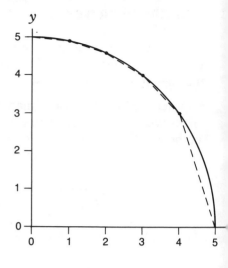

C3 (a) Explain why the point where x is 2·5 is one-third of the way along the length of the quarter-circle from (0, 5) to (5, 0).

(b) The straight-lines approximation to the curve is much 'closer' to the curve between $x = 0$ and $x = 2·5$ than between $x = 2·5$ and $x = 5$. Calculate an approximation to the length of the curve based only on the piece from $x = 0$ to $x = 2·5$ using steps of 0·5 in x. Compare your result with the length as calculated using π.

C4 Which of the three paths below gives the best approximation to the straight-line distance from P to Q?

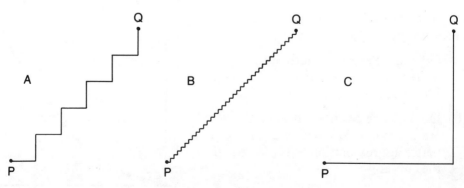

4 Quadratic functions

A A function program

Here is a program for calculating the values of a function f, using an electronic calculator.

> 1 Enter x.
> 2 Subtract 7 (then press =).
> 3 Square.
> 4 Add 16 (then press =).
> 5 Write down the value of $f(x)$.

1 (a) Use the program to work out the values of $f(x)$ needed to complete this table.

x	0	2	4	6	8	10	12	14
$f(x)$	65							

(b) Check on your calculator that $f(3) = 32$. Look carefully at the completed table in part (a), and guess another value of x for which $f(x) = 32$. Check that your guess is correct.

2 The table in question A1 shows that $f(x)$ decreases as x goes up to 6 and increases as x goes up from 8. Find the minimum value of $f(x)$.

3 Draw the graph of the function f for values of x from 0 to 14.
(Use a scale of 1 cm to 2 on the x-axis and 1 cm to 5 on the y-axis.)

Draw the line of reflection symmetry of the graph, and label it with its equation.

4 The function f can be written in the form $x \to (x - \ldots)^2 + \ldots$
Write it in this form.

Here is the graph of the function f.

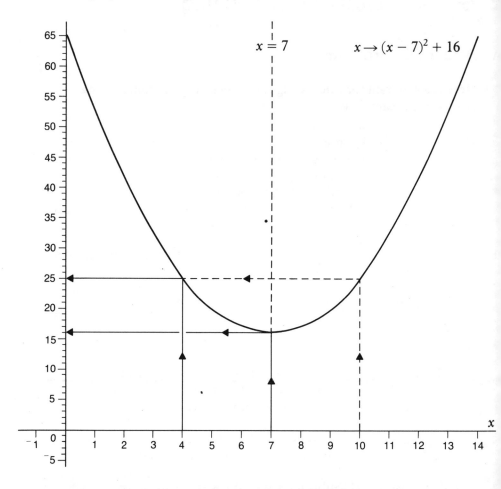

The graph is symmetrical about the line $x = 7$.
The minimum value of $f(x)$ is 16, and this occurs when x is 7.

The graph is symmetrical about $x = 7$ because there are pairs of values of x on either side of 7 which give the same value of $f(x)$.
For example, 4 is **3 less than 7**, and 10 is **3 more than 7**; and $f(4)$ and $f(10)$ are both equal to 25.

5 Use the formula $f(x) = (x - 7)^2 + 16$ to explain why
   (a) the minimum value of $f(x)$ is 16
   (b) the values of $f(4)$ and $f(10)$ are equal

6 Check by calculation that $f(8 \cdot 5) = 18 \cdot 25$.
   Which other value of x also gives a value of $f(x)$ equal to $18 \cdot 25$?
   Check by calculation.

7 Check by calculation that $f(20) = 185$.
   For which other value of x is $f(x)$ also equal to 185? Check by calculation.

8 Two values of x which are equally spaced either side of 7 can be written in the form $7 - a$ and $7 + a$, where a is any number.

   Use the formula $f(x) = (x - 7)^2 + 16$ to explain why it is that $f(7 + a)$ and $f(7 - a)$ must be equal.

9 Write down (i) the equation of the line of symmetry of the graph
              (ii) the minimum value of the function
   for each of the functions given below. Try to do this without actually drawing the graphs or making tables of values, if you can.
   (a) $x \to (x - 3)^2 + 8$ (b) $x \to (x - 1)^2 + 5$ (c) $x \to (x - 35)^2 + 29$

10 This is a program for calculating values of a function g.

   > 1 Enter x.
   > 2 Add 5 (and press =).
   > 3 Square.
   > 4 Subtract 8 (and press =).
   > 5 Write down the value of $g(x)$.

   (a) Write this function in the form $x \to \ldots$
   (b) Before you draw the graph, write down what you think is the equation of its line of symmetry, and the minimum value of $g(x)$.
   (c) Draw the graph for values of x from 0 to 10, and check your answers to part (b).

B Translating graphs

Here is a table of values of x, $x - 3$ and $(x - 3)^2$ for values of x from 0 to 7.

x	0	1	2	3	4	5	6	7
$x - 3$	−3	−2	−1	0	1	2	3	4
$(x - 3)^2$	9	4	1	0	1	4	9	16

The graph of $x \to (x - 3)^2$ looks like this.

It looks like the graph of $x \to x^2$, but is shifted 3 units to the right. Its line of symmetry is $x = 3$.

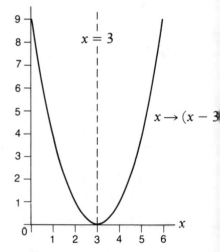

In the diagram here you can see that we get the graph of $x \to (x - 3)^2$ by **translating** the graph of $x \to x^2$ **3 units to the right.**

Notice that the lowest point, or **vertex**, of the graph of $x \to x^2$ is where x is 0.

The vertex of the graph of $x \to (x - 3)^2$ is where $x - 3$ is 0.

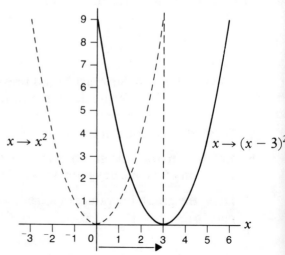

For the work which follows you need tracing paper.

In the following questions use a scale of 1 cm to 1 unit on each axis.

1. Draw the graph of $x \to x^2$ by plotting values of $x = {}^-3, {}^-2\cdot 5, {}^-2, {}^-1\cdot 5$, etc. up to 3. Draw the graph as accurately as you can.

   Trace the graph itself only (**not** the axes) on tracing paper. You will need the tracing for the questions which follow.

2. (a) Make a table of values of the function $x \to (x + 5)^2$ for values of x from $^-8$ to $^-2$. Draw the graph of $x \to (x + 5)^2$.

   (b) Use your tracing to find what translation has to be given to the graph of $x \to x^2$ to get the graph of $x \to (x + 5)^2$.

3. (a) Calculate the values of the function $x \to x^2 - 6$ for values of x from $^-3$ to 3, and draw the graph of $x \to x^2 - 6$.

   (b) What translation of the graph of $x \to x^2$ will give the graph of $x \to x^2 - 6$?

4. The graph of the function

   $$x \to (x - 7)^2 + 2$$

   can be obtained from that of $x \to x^2$ by a horizontal translation and a vertical translation.

   (a) Before you draw the graph of $x \to (x - 7)^2 + 2$, describe the horizontal translation (and say whether it is to the left or right) and the vertical translation (and say whether it is up or down).

   (b) Draw the graph of $x \to (x - 7)^2 + 2$ for values of x from 4 to 10, and check your answers to part (a).

5. State the horizontal and vertical translations which have to be given to the graph of $x \to x^2$ to get each of these graphs.

   (a) $x \to x^2 - 8$ (b) $x \to (x - 8)^2$ (c) $x \to (x + 10)^2$
   (d) $x \to x^2 + 3$ (e) $x \to (x - 9)^2 - 2$ (f) $x \to (x + 12)^2 + 14$
   (g) $x \to (x - a)^2 + b$ (h) $x \to (x + a)^2 + b$ (i) $x \to (x + a)^2 - b$

B6 The graph of each of these functions is one of the graphs below. Which graph goes with each function?

(a) $x \to (x-2)^2 - 1$ (b) $x \to (x-1)^2 - 2$ (c) $x \to (x+1)^2 + 2$
(d) $x \to (x+2)^2 - 1$ (e) $x \to (x-1)^2 + 2$ (f) $x \to (x+1)^2 - 2$
(g) $x \to (x-2)^2 + 1$ (h) $x \to (x+2)^2 + 1$

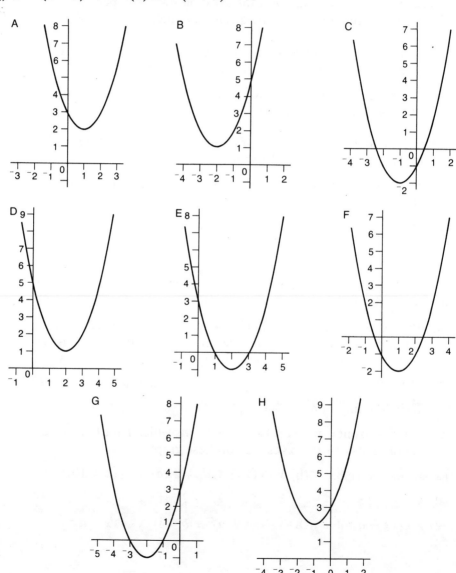

C Completing the square

All the functions we have looked at so far in this chapter have been written in the form

$$x \to (x+p)^2 + q$$

where p and q are numbers, which may be positive or negative.

Any function which can be written in the form above can also be written in the form

$$x \to x^2 + bx + c$$

For example, take the function $x \to (x-5)^2 - 13$. We can multiply out $(x-5)^2$ in the usual way:

$$(x-5)^2 = (x-5)(x-5) = x^2 - 5x - 5x + 25$$
$$= x^2 - 10x + 25.$$

It follows that $x \to (x-5)^2 - 13$
can be written as $x \to (x^2 - 10x + 25) - 13$
or $x \to x^2 - 10x + 12$.

1 Write each of these functions in the form $x \to x^2 + bx + c$.

(a) $x \to (x+4)^2 - 1$
(b) $x \to (x-3)^2 + 1$
(c) $x \to (x+8)^2 - 64$
(d) $x \to (x-10)^2 - 101$
(e) $x \to (x+15)^2 - 25$
(f) $x \to (x+1)^2 - 9$
(g) $x \to (x-7)^2 + 1$
(h) $x \to (x-0\cdot5)^2 + 1\cdot75$
(i) $x \to (x-3\cdot5)^2 - 1\cdot25$

2 (a) Write the function $x \to (x+4)^2 + 3$ in the form $x \to x^2 + bx + c$.

(b) Use the answer to part (a) to help you write each of these in the form $x \to (x+p)^2 + q$
   (i) $x \to x^2 + 8x + 20$
   (ii) $x \to x^2 + 8x + 14$
   (iii) $x \to x^2 + 8x$

3 Use some of the answers to question C1 to help you write each of these in the form $x \to (x+p)^2 + q$.

(a) $x \to x^2 - 6x + 15$
(b) $x \to x^2 - 20x + 5$
(c) $x \to x^2 + 2x - 20$

On the previous page we saw that the function $x \to (x-5)^2 - 13$ can be written in the form $x \to x^2 - 10x + 12$.

For many purposes, the form $x \to (x-5)^2 - 13$ is more useful.

For example, from this form we can visualise the graph straight away. It is the graph of $x \to x^2$, translated 5 units to the right and 13 units down.

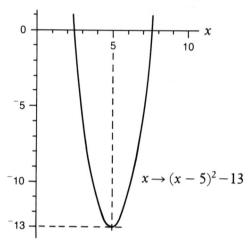

$x \to (x-5)^2 - 13$

So the problem arises: if we have the function in the form $x \to x^2 - 10x + 12$, how do we get it into the form $x \to (x-5)^2 - 13$?

The method depends on knowing what we get when we multiply out an expression of the form $(x + p)^2$.

$$(x + p)^2 = (x + p)(x + p) = x^2 + px + px + p^2 = x^2 + 2px + p^2$$

As we shall see in a moment, the important things here are the term x^2 and the term $2px$.

It is important to know that, for example,

$(x + 7)^2$ starts $x^2 + 14x + \ldots$

$(x - 8)^2$ starts $x^2 - 16x + \ldots$

$(x + 2 \cdot 5)^2$ starts $x^2 + 5x + \ldots$

$(x - 3 \cdot 5)^2$ starts $x^2 - 7x + \ldots$

and so on.

So if we have a function in the form $x \to x^2 - 10x + 12$, we look at the first two terms, $x^2 - 10x$, and we think

$$\text{'}(x-5)^2 \text{ starts } x^2 - 10x + \ldots\text{'}$$

So we multiply out $(x - 5)^2$ to get $x^2 - 10x + 25$.

What we actually want is $x^2 - 10x + 12$, so we have to subtract 13 from $x^2 - 10x + 25$.

So $x^2 - 10x + 12 = \underbrace{(x - 5)^2}_{x^2 - 10x + 25} - 13$

This method of going from an expression in the form $x^2 + bx + c$ to an equivalent expression in the form $(x + p)^2 + q$ is called **completing the square**.

Here is another example of completing the square.

Worked example

Express $x^2 + 6x + 14$ in the form $(x + p)^2 + q$.

We look at $x^2 + 6x$ and think '$(x + 3)^2$ starts $x^2 + 6x + \ldots$'

So we multiply out $(x + 3)^2$ to get $x^2 + 6x + 9$.

What we want is $x^2 + 6x + 14$ so we have to add 5 to $x^2 + 6x + 9$.

So $x^2 + 6x + 14 = (x + 3)^2 + 5$.

Write each of these functions in the form $x \to (x + p)^2 + q$.
(a) $x \to x^2 + 14x + 50$ (b) $x \to x^2 - 6x + 12$ (c) $x \to x^2 + 8x + 16$
(d) $x \to x^2 - 26x + 170$ (e) $x \to x^2 + 5x + 5 \cdot 25$ (f) $x \to x^2 - 9x + 20$
(g) $x \to x^2 + x + 7$ (h) $x \to x^2 - x - 1$ (i) $x \to x^2 - \frac{1}{2}x + 1$

For each function in question C4, write down
 (i) the equation of the line of symmetry of the graph
(ii) the minimum value of the function

D Quadratic equations

This is the graph of the function

$$f(x) = (x-5)^2 - 9$$

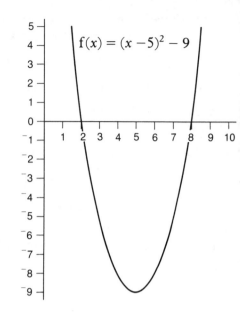

There are two points on the graph where $f(x) = 0$.
They are the two points where the graph crosses the x-axis.

The values of x at these two points are 2 and 8.
So $x = 2$ and $x = 8$ are the two solutions of the equation $f(x) = 0$, or

$$(x-5)^2 - 9 = 0.$$

It is not necessary to draw the graph to find the solutions of the equation $(x-5)^2 - 9 = 0$. The equation can be solved by algebra, like this.

Add 9 to both sides.

$$(x-5)^2 - 9 = 0$$
$$(x-5)^2 = 9$$

At this point we take the square root of both sides. You might be tempted to write down '$x - 5 = 3$' because 3 is the square root of 9.

But you have to remember that there are in fact **two** 'square roots' of 9. One is 3, and the other is $^-3$, because $(^-3)^2$ is also 9.

Either $x - 5 = 3$ or $x - 5 = {}^-3$

So either $x = 8$ or $x = 2$

D1 Solve these equations.
(a) $(x-4)^2 - 25 = 0$ (b) $(x+2)^2 - 36 = 0$ (c) $(x+10)^2 - 16 = 0$

38

In the next example, the square roots are not whole numbers. But, as before, both positive and negative square roots have to be included.

Worked example

Solve the equation $(x - 3)^2 - 5 = 0$.

$$(x - 3)^2 - 5 = 0$$
$$(x - 3)^2 = 5$$
$$x - 3 = \sqrt{5} \text{ or } x - 3 = -\sqrt{5}$$
$$x = 3 + \sqrt{5} \text{ or } x = 3 - \sqrt{5}$$

Notice that $\sqrt{5}$ has been left in its exact form. It could easily be replaced by a decimal approximation, for example 2·236 (to 3 d.p.).

Notice also that the negative root of 5 is written as $^-\sqrt{5}$. Its value to 3 decimal places is $^-2·236$.

We can write the pair of solutions in the form $x = 3 \pm \sqrt{5}$. We read this as '3 plus or minus $\sqrt{5}$'.

(To 3 decimal places the two solutions are $3 + 2·236$ and $3 - 2·236$, that is 5·236 and 1·764.)

This diagram shows how the two solutions are related to the graph of $x \to (x - 3)^2 - 5$.

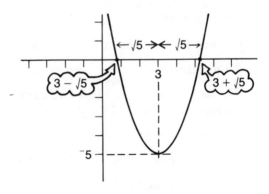

Solve each of these equations. Write each pair of solutions in the form $x = a \pm \sqrt{b}$, and calculate them to 2 decimal places.

(a) $(x - 7)^2 - 3 = 0$ (b) $(x + 2)^2 - 6 = 0$ (c) $(x + 1)^2 - 2 = 0$
(d) $(x - 5)^2 - 5 = 0$ (e) $(x + 6)^2 - 8 = 0$ (f) $(x - 2)^2 - 10 = 0$

If we try to solve the equation $(x - 3)^2 + 5 = 0$ we come up against a problem.

$$(x - 3)^2 + 5 = 0$$
$$(x - 3)^2 = {}^-5$$

> The square of a number cannot be negative. So the equation has no solution.

D3 Draw the graph of $x \rightarrow (x - 3)^2 + 5$. What feature of the graph shows that the equation $(x - 3)^2 + 5 = 0$ has no solution?

D4 Solve the equation $(x - 3)^2 = 0$. How many solutions does the equation have? What special feature of the graph of $x \rightarrow (x - 3)^2$ shows this?

To solve an equation of the form $x^2 + bx + c = 0$, we first write it in the form $(x + p)^2 + q = 0$ by completing the square.

Worked example

Solve the equation $x^2 + 10x - 15 = 0$.

(1) The first step is to re-write the expression $x^2 + 10x - 15$ in the form $(x + p)^2 + q$.

We look at $x^2 + 10x$ and think '$(x + 5)^2$ starts $x^2 + 10x + \ldots$'

We multiply out $(x + 5)^2$ and get $x^2 + 10x + 25$.

We want $x^2 + 10x - 15$, so we have to subtract 40 from $x^2 + 10x + 25$, because $x^2 + 10x + 25 - 40 = x^2 + 10x - 15$.

So $x^2 + 10x - 15 = (x + 5)^2 - 40$.

(2) Re-write the equation $x^2 + 10x - 15 = 0$ as $(x + 5)^2 - 40 = 0$.

Then solve the equation.
$$(x + 5)^2 - 40 = 0$$
$$(x + 5)^2 = 40$$
$$x + 5 = \pm\sqrt{40}$$
$$\boldsymbol{x = {}^-5 \pm \sqrt{40}}$$

(To 2 d.p., $x = {}^-5 \pm 6\cdot32 = 1\cdot32$ or $^-11\cdot32$.)

Solve each of these equations. Write each pair of solutions in the form $x = a \pm \sqrt{b}$ and calculate them to 2 d.p.

(a) $x^2 - 10x + 15 = 0$ (b) $x^2 - 4x - 4 = 0$ (c) $x^2 + 16x + 14 = 0$
(d) $x^2 - 24x + 138 = 0$ (e) $x^2 + 20x + 98 = 0$ (f) $x^2 + 6x + 7\cdot5 = 0$
(g) $x^2 - 0\cdot4x - 2 = 0$ (h) $x^2 - 3\cdot2x + 2 = 0$ (i) $x^2 + \frac{7}{6}x - 3 = 0$

So far all the quadratic equations we have solved have been of the form $x^2 + bx + c = 0$.

The equation $10 + 4x - x^2 = 0$ is also a quadratic equation. We can change it to the form $x^2 + bx + c = 0$ by **multiplying both sides by ⁻1**.

$$10 + 4x - x^2 = 0$$

Multiply both sides by ⁻1. $^{-}(10 + 4x - x^2) = 0$

Remove brackets. $^{-}10 - 4x + x^2 = 0$

or $x^2 - 4x - 10 = 0$

Solve the equation $10 + 4x - x^2 = 0$, correct to 2 d.p.

Solve each of these equations, correct to 2 d.p.

(a) $8 - 3x - x^2 = 0$ (b) $2 + 6x - x^2 = 0$ (c) $15 + 10x - x^2 = 0$

We can solve the equation $2x^2 - 12x - 5 = 0$ by first dividing both sides by 2.

$$2x^2 - 12x - 5 = 0$$
Divide both sides by 2. $x^2 - 6x - 2\cdot5 = 0$

Find the solutions of $2x^2 - 12x - 5 = 0$, to 2 d.p.

Solve each of these equations, correct to 2 d.p.

(a) $2x^2 - 8x - 3 = 0$ (b) $3x^2 + 6x - 15 = 0$ (c) $20 + 16x - 5x^2 = 0$

Investigate the solutions of the equation $x^6 - 35x^3 + 216 = 0$.

5 Random devices

A A dice

Dice were used for games of chance in ancient Egypt. It is possible that dice-like objects such as the talus (the heel-bone of a sheep or deer), which can land in four different ways when thrown, were used by older civilisations than Egypt.

Talus

Dice are used for games of chance because they are unpredictable. We also expect a dice to be fair: each of the six numbers should be equally likely to come up. In a long run of throws we expect all six numbers to come up with roughly equal frequencies.

A dice, a coin being tossed and a roulette wheel are all examples of what are called 'random devices'.

We often ask people to think of a name or number 'at random' or to choose a card 'at random'. But this may produce results very different from those which, say, a dice or roulette wheel would give, because people have certain numbers that they prefer and other numbers that they avoid.

Pick a c -any ca

A1 How good are you at being a dice?

Try this experiment.

(a) Imagine that you are rolling a fair dice 200 times. Write down the sequence of 'scores' (1 to 6) that you imagine coming up. It is a good idea to write your scores on ten lines with twenty on each line, to keep track of how many 'throws' you have had.

(b) Count the number of 1s, the number of 2s, etc. in your 200 scores. (A tally table is one way of doing this.) The frequencies should, of course, add up to 200.

With a fair dice all six scores are equally likely, and in a very long run of throws (say 1000 or more) you would expect the frequency of each score to be close to $\frac{1}{6}$ of the total number of throws. But in a series as short as 200 throws some scores may come up quite a bit more often than others, even with a fair dice.

Look at the frequencies in your table. If they mostly lie between 28 and 38, you have represented the scores in roughly the proportion that a real dice usually does.[1]

But getting roughly equal frequencies for each score is not the only test of whether someone is producing numbers like a real dice. Many people feel that when a throw of a dice produces a certain score, then that particular score is less likely to come up at the next throw. For example, if a 4 has come up, they think that the next throw is more likely to give 1, 2, 3, 5 or 6 than another 4. So when they are asked to imagine the sequence of scores which a dice would produce, they have a tendency to avoid putting a 4 straight after a 4, or a 1 straight after a 1, etc.

But a dice does not have a memory. What has happened in previous throws cannot affect the outcome of its next throw. If a 4 has come up, the next number is just as likely to be a 4 as any other number. We say the result of each throw is **independent** of the results of earlier throws.

2   Here are the results of 200 throws of a real dice. Each **repeat** is marked with a dash.

```
2 4 6–6 1 2 5 6 2 6 2 3–3 6 4 2 6 2 4 2
4–4–4 5 1–1 5 4 5 2 4 6–6 4 1 2 4 1–1 6
2 5 3 2 6 3 5 1–1 4 5 6 2 1 5 4 1 2 4 1
2–2 1 3 4 5 2 6 3 5 3 1 4 1 2–2–2 3 4–4–
4 6 4–4 2 1 6 5 6–6 1 2–2–2 6 1 2 3 5 1
4 5 3 1 6 2–2 1–1 3 5–5 6 3 6 2 1 3 5–5
6 1 3 1 2 3–3 4 2 5 2 1 6 2 1 3 1–1 4 1
5 2 6 3 2 3 1 3 6 5 6 1–1–1 2 1 6 2 3–3–
3–3 4 1 3 6 1 3–3 1 5 1 4 3 2 3 2 4–4 6
5 6 1 4–4 5–5–5 3 6 5 6 5–5 4–4 3 5 1 3
```

There are 35 repeats, which is fairly typical for a real dice.

Count the repeats in your own sequence and compare.

---

[1] Even with a fair dice it is **possible** to get extremely unequal frequencies, such as, say, 100 sixes, 100 fives and nothing else. But such an occurrence is extremely unlikely.

B A coin

On the opposite page there are three sequences, P, Q and R. Each sequence has 600 numbers in it. 1 stands for a head; 0 stands for a tail.

One of the sequences has been produced by tossing a fair coin.
One has been produced by a person 'pretending to be a coin'.
One has been produced by a 'random number generator' on a computer.

The challenge is to see if we can tell which sequence is which.

First we can count the 0s and 1s in each sequence. The results are:

Sequence P	Sequence Q	Sequence R
0: 296 **1:** 304	**0:** 303 **1:** 297	**0:** 304 **1:** 296

In each case there are about half heads and half tails. So all three sequences behave like real coins as far as the frequency of heads and tails is concerned.

We know that the outcome of a throw of a real coin is independent of the outcome of the previous throw. If one throw is 0, the next throw is equally likely to be 0 or 1. So if we pick out all the 0s in a long sequence and look at the next throw in each case, we should get 0s and 1s with about equal frequency.

B1 (a) Go through the first two lines of sequence P. Each time you come to a 0, note down whether it is followed by 0 or by 1, and make a tally.

		Frequency
0 followed by 0	|| etc.	
0 followed by 1	||| etc.	

(b) Make a similar tally for 1 followed by 0 and 1 followed by 1 in the first two lines of sequence P.

B2 Repeat question B1 for sequences Q and R.

Which sequence seems most 'un-coin-like'?

Sequence P

1 0 0 1 0 1 1 1 0 1 0 1 1 0 1 1 0 1 1 1 1 1 0 1 0 0 0 1 0 0 0 0 1 1 0 1 1 0 1 1
1 0 0 0 0 0 1 1 1 1 0 1 1 0 1 0 0 1 0 0 1 0 0 0 1 0 0 1 1 1 0 0 0 1 1 0 0 0 1 0
1 1 0 0 0 0 0 1 1 0 1 1 0 1 0 0 1 0 0 1 1 0 1 1 1 0 1 0 0 1 0 1 0 0 1 1 0 0 0 1
1 0 0 0 0 0 1 1 1 0 1 0 1 1 1 1 0 0 1 1 0 1 0 1 0 0 1 0 1 0 1 0 0 1 0 0 0 0 0 1
0 1 1 0 0 1 0 1 0 0 1 0 0 1 0 1 1 1 1 0 0 1 0 1 1 1 0 0 1 0 1 1 0 1 0 1 0 1 0 0
0 0 1 0 0 0 1 0 1 1 1 1 0 0 0 1 1 0 0 1 1 0 0 0 0 1 0 0 1 1 1 0 1 0 0 0 1 0 0 0
1 0 0 1 1 1 0 1 0 1 0 1 0 1 1 1 1 0 0 0 0 0 0 1 0 0 0 0 1 1 1 1 1 1 1 1 0 1 0
1 1 1 1 1 0 1 0 0 0 1 1 1 1 0 0 0 1 1 0 1 1 1 0 1 0 1 0 0 1 1 1 1 1 0 1 1 1 0
0 0 0 0 0 1 0 1 1 1 1 0 0 1 0 0 1 1 1 1 0 1 0 1 0 0 1 0 0 0 1 0 1 0 1 0 1 0 1 0
1 0 1 0 1 1 0 0 0 1 1 1 0 0 1 1 0 0 0 1 1 1 0 0 0 1 0 1 0 1 1 0 0 0 1 1 1 1 0 0
1 1 1 1 0 0 1 1 0 0 0 0 1 1 0 1 1 1 0 1 0 1 1 1 1 0 1 0 1 1 0 0 0 1 0 0 0 1 1 0
0 1 1 0 0 0 1 1 0 1 1 0 1 0 1 1 1 1 0 1 0 1 1 1 0 0 1 1 1 0 1 0 1 0 0 0 0 1
1 0 0 0 0 0 0 1 0 0 0 1 0 1 0 1 1 1 1 1 1 1 0 1 1 1 0 0 0 0 1 0 0 0 0 1 1 0 1 0
1 0 1 1 0 1 1 1 0 1 1 0 0 1 1 0 1 1 1 0 0 0 1 0 1 1 0 1 0 1 1 0 1 1 0 1 0 1 1 1
0 0 0 0 0 1 1 0 0 1 0 0 0 0 1 0 0 1 0 1 0 0 1 0 1 1 0 0 0 1 1 1 0 1 1 0 1 1 1 1

Sequence Q

0 0 1 1 0 0 1 0 1 0 0 0 1 0 0 0 1 1 1 1 0 0 0 1 0 0 0 1 0 0 1 0 1 0 1 1 1 0 1 0
1 1 1 0 1 0 1 1 0 1 1 0 1 0 0 1 1 0 1 1 0 1 0 1 1 0 1 1 0 1 0 1 0 1 0 1 1 0 1 0
1 0 1 0 1 0 1 0 1 0 0 0 1 1 0 1 1 1 0 1 0 0 1 0 0 1 1 0 1 0 0 0 0 1 0 1 0 1 0 0
1 0 1 0 1 0 0 1 0 1 0 1 0 1 0 1 1 0 0 1 0 1 0 1 0 1 0 1 1 1 0 1 0 1 1 0 1 1 1 0
1 0 1 0 0 1 0 1 0 0 1 0 1 0 1 0 1 1 0 0 0 0 1 0 0 1 0 1 0 1 0 1 0 1 1 1 0 1 0 1
0 1 1 0 1 0 0 1 0 0 1 0 1 1 0 1 1 0 1 0 1 0 1 0 1 0 1 1 0 0 1 1 0 1 0 1 0 1 0 1
0 1 1 0 1 1 0 0 1 0 1 1 0 1 0 0 1 0 0 0 1 0 1 1 0 1 1 1 0 0 0 1 1 1 1 1 0 0 0
1 0 0 1 0 1 1 0 1 0 1 1 1 1 0 1 0 0 1 0 0 0 0 0 1 1 1 0 0 1 0 1 0 1 0 1 1 1 0 1
1 0 1 0 1 1 1 0 0 1 1 0 1 0 1 0 1 0 0 1 0 1 0 0 0 1 1 0 1 1 0 1 0 0 1 1 0 1 0 1
0 1 0 1 0 1 0 1 0 1 0 0 1 0 0 1 0 0 0 1 1 0 1 0 1 1 1 0 0 1 0 1 1 0 0 1 0 1
0 1 0 0 1 1 1 0 1 0 0 1 1 0 1 1 1 0 1 0 1 0 1 0 1 0 0 1 0 0 1 0 1 0 1 0 1 0
1 0 1 0 0 1 0 0 1 1 0 1 0 1 0 1 0 0 1 0 0 0 0 1 0 1 0 1 1 1 0 1 0 1 0 0 0 0 1 1
0 0 1 0 0 0 1 1 0 1 0 0 1 0 1 0 1 0 1 0 1 1 1 0 0 1 0 1 0 1 0 0 1 0 1 0 1 0 1 1
0 0 0 1 0 1 0 1 0 1 0 1 0 0 1 0 1 0 1 0 1 0 1 0 1 0 1 0 1 1 1 0 1 1 0 1 0 0 1 1
0 1 0 0 1 0 0 0 1 1 0 0 1 0 1 0 0 1 0 1 1 0 0 1 0 0 1 0 1 1 0 1 0 0 1 0 0 1 1 0

Sequence R

0 1 0 1 1 1 1 0 0 1 1 1 1 0 0 0 1 0 0 0 0 1 0 0 0 0 0 0 0 1 1 0 0 0 1 0 1 0
0 1 1 1 0 0 0 0 1 1 1 0 1 1 0 1 0 0 1 1 0 1 1 0 1 0 1 1 1 0 1 1 0 1 1 1 0 0 1
0 1 1 1 0 0 1 1 1 0 0 0 0 1 0 0 0 0 1 1 1 0 1 1 0 1 0 0 0 1 0 1 0 1 1 0 1 0 0 1
1 1 1 0 1 0 1 1 1 1 0 0 0 0 1 0 1 1 1 0 0 1 0 1 0 1 0 1 0 1 1 0 1 0 1 1 1 0 1 0
1 1 0 1 0 0 1 1 0 0 0 1 1 1 1 1 1 0 0 1 1 0 1 1 0 1 0 1 0 1 1 1 1 0 0 0 1 1 1
0 0 1 1 1 0 1 0 0 0 1 0 1 1 0 0 0 0 0 1 1 1 0 1 1 1 0 0 0 0 1 0 1 1 0 0 0 0 1 0
1 0 1 0 0 0 1 0 1 1 0 0 1 0 0 1 0 0 1 1 1 1 0 1 0 1 1 1 0 0 0 0 0 1 0 1 1 0 0 1 0
0 1 1 1 1 1 0 1 0 1 1 0 1 1 0 0 0 0 1 1 1 0 0 1 0 1 0 1 1 0 1 0 1 1 0 0 0 0 0 0
1 0 0 1 1 1 1 1 1 1 0 0 1 0 0 1 0 0 0 0 1 1 0 0 1 0 0 0 1 0 0 0 0 0 1 1 0 0 1 0
1 0 0 0 0 0 0 1 0 1 1 1 0 1 1 0 1 1 1 0 1 1 0 0 1 1 0 1 0 0 0 1 1 0 1 0 1 0 1 0
1 1 1 0 0 0 0 0 0 1 0 0 1 0 0 0 0 1 1 0 0 0 0 1 1 1 0 0 1 1 0 1 0 1 0 0 1 0 1 1
1 0 0 0 0 1 1 1 0 1 1 1 1 0 1 1 1 1 0 1 0 0 0 1 0 1 0 0 1 1 0 0 0 0 1 1 1 0 0
1 0 0 1 0 0 0 1 1 0 0 1 1 1 0 0 0 1 1 1 0 0 1 0 1 0 1 0 1 0 0 1 1 1 1 1 0 1 0
1 1 0 1 1 1 1 0 0 0 1 0 0 0 0 1 0 0 0 1 1 1 1 0 1 1 0 0 0 1 0 1 0 1 1 1 0 0 1
1 1 0 1 0 1 1 0 0 0 0 0 1 0 1 1 1 0 0 1 0 1 0 0 0 0 1 0 1 1 0 1 0 1 1 0 0 0 0 1

Runs

When a coin comes up the same way a number of times, we say there is a 'run' of heads, or a 'run' of tails.
Here are some examples of runs.

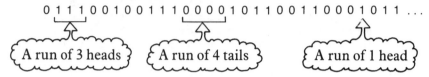

A 'run of 1 head' means an isolated head preceded by a tail and followed by a tail.

Think of a sequence being produced by a real fair coin. Each throw (apart from the first one) will either be the same as the previous one or different from it, and these two outcomes are equally likely.
So, in a long sequence of throws, we would expect about half the throws to be the same as the previous throw, and about half to be different from the previous throw.

But every time a throw is different from the previous throw, a new run starts. For example, in the sequence below, throws which are different from their predecessors are marked with a dot. Each one is the start of a new run.

$$0\,1\,1\,\dot{0}\,\dot{1}\,1\,1\,\dot{0}\,0\,0\,\dot{1}\,\dot{1}\,0\,\dot{1}\,1\,0\,0\,0\,\dot{1}\,\dot{0}\,\dot{1}\,1\,1\,\dot{0}\,\dot{1}\,\dot{0}\,0\,0\,\dot{1}\,1\,\ldots$$

So the number of runs is equal to the number of throws which are different from their predecessors. In the case of a real fair coin, about half of all the throws are expected to be different from their predecessors. So, in the case of a real coin, the number of **runs** is expected to be about half the number of **throws** in the sequence. (For example, a sequence of 200 throws is expected to contain about 100 runs.)

If the number of runs in a sequence of 0s and 1s is a lot different from half of the number of throws, then we would suspect that the sequence was not produced by a real coin.

B3 Use the 'number of runs test' to find out whether this sequence of 100 'throws' is behaving like a real coin.

1011110000011011000111001101100111011101101111000

0011101100001101011011100110111000001011010110 1011

Further tests

It is possible to have a sequence which is very un-coin-like, but which passes all the tests so far. An example occurs in the next question.

B4 Look at this **repeating** sequences: 0 0 1 1 0 0 1 1 0 0 1 1 0 0 1 1 ...
Explain why this sequence passes each of these tests:

(a) 0 and 1 occur with equal frequency.

(b) 0 is followed by 0 as often as it is followed by 1.

(c) 1 is followed by 0 and 1 with equal frequency.

(d) The number of runs is about half the number of throws.

The sequence 0 0 1 1 0 0 1 1 0 0 1 1 ... is predictable, and not coin-like at all. The pair 00 is always followed by a 1, whereas in a real coin sequence 00 would be followed by 0 about as often as it is followed by 1. Similarly 01 would be followed by 0 and 1 with roughly equal frequency, and so on.

B5 Here again is the sequence in question B3, with all the 00 pairs marked. How many of them are followed by 0 and how many by 1? Does the sequence pass this test?

1 0 1 1 1 1 0̂0̂0̂0̂0̂ 1 1 0 1 1 0̂0̂ 1 1 1 0̂0̂ 1 1 0 1 1 0̂0̂ 1 1 1 0 1 1 1 0 1 1 0 1 1 1 1 0̂0̂

0̂0̂ 1 1 1 0 1 1 0̂0̂ 1 1 0 1 0 1 1 0 1 1 1 0̂0̂ 1 1 0 1 1 1 0̂0̂0̂0̂ 1 0 1 1 0 1 0 1 1 0 1 0 1 1

B6 Challenge! Try to find a **repeating** sequence in which the pair 00 is followed by 0 and 1 with equal frequency, and the same is true of the pairs 01, 10 and 11. Does your sequence pass the other tests in this chapter?

Problems and investigations (2)

1 Four large cylinders and four small cylinders are placed on the board shown on the right.

   Each row contains one large and one small. Each column contains one large and one small.

   The views in the direction of the arrows A and B are shown below.

   Find all the possible ways in which the cylinders may be arranged on the board to give these two views.

2 This is a side view of a garden roller.

   Calculate the radius of the roller.

   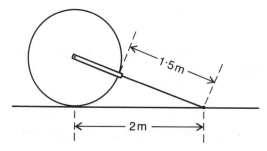

3 At what times of day is the angle between the two hands of a clock
   (a) 180°   (b) 90°

4 Two pegs, A and B, are fixed, and a '30-60-90' set-square is placed between them, as shown here. The set-square is moved so that two edges slide against the pegs.

What is the locus of the vertex V?

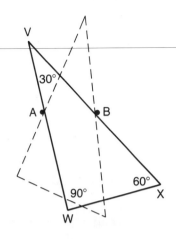

If the set-square is moved until vertex V reaches peg A, . . .

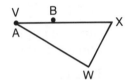

. . . then V can go through the gap between the pegs. Afterwards the edge VX slides against both pegs.

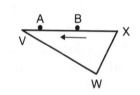

When vertex X reaches peg B, it can go through the gap, so that the edges VX and XW now slide against the pegs.

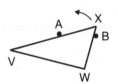

This movement can continue until the set-square is back in a position where the edges VW and VX slide against the pegs.

Draw the locus of V during this complete movement.

Investigate what can happen if the gap AB is increased.

49

6 Logic puzzles (1)

1 **The broken window puzzle**

After school one day, a window is broken in the playground. There were only five pupils playing there at the time – Sandra, Paul, Wendy, Ted and Angela.

When the headmaster questions them, this is what they say:

> Sandra: 'It was Paul.'
> Wendy: 'It wasn't me.'
> Paul: 'Ted did it.'
> Ted: 'Paul is lying.'
> Angela: 'It definitely wasn't me or Wendy.'

Only **one** pupil is telling the truth and nothing but the truth. Who broke the window?

Have a good try at solving this puzzle. If you cannot get anywhere with it, or if you have an answer but are not sure of it, turn to page 63 for some suggestions.

When you have solved the broken window puzzle (either entirely by yourself or with the help of the suggestions), have a go at solving this one:

2 **The sports day puzzle**

Four children have a race.
Afterwards, this is what they tell their friends:

> Brenda: 'Peter finished in front of me and Neil was just behind me.'
> Sally: 'Neil won the race and I beat Peter.'
> Neil: 'Brenda was just behind me when I finished.'
> Peter: 'I came in second, ahead of the two girls.'

Only **two** people are telling the truth, the winner and one other person.

In what order did the four children finish the race?

7 Polygons and polyhedra

A Trigonometry

Suppose you want to calculate the length marked x in this right-angled triangle.

x is the side opposite the angle of 36°.
You know that the hypotenuse is 2 units.
So you would use the sine of 36°.

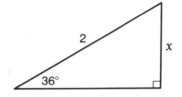

$x = 2 \sin 36°$

At this point you would probably reach for your calculator, and use it to work out $2 \sin 36°$. You would probably write down something like this:

$x = 1 \cdot 18$ (to 2 d.p.)

For most practical purposes, this would be quite satisfactory. But there are two reasons why it is sometimes better to keep the **exact** answer of '$x = 2 \sin 36°$'.

First, the value of $\sin 36°$ which a calculator gives is only approximate, no matter how many decimal places it gives.
Second, the answer '$x = 1 \cdot 18$' gives no clue as to where this number came from. If later on you need to work out $\dfrac{x}{\sin 36°}$ you would probably not realise that the answer should be exactly 2.

In this chapter, write all answers in an exact form, like $2 \sin 36°$, or $\sqrt{5}$ for example. Do not use a calculator at all.

An answer like '$x = 2 \sin 36°$' may appear strange and 'unfinished' at first. But you know that if ever you wanted to convert it into an approximate numerical form, you could do so quite easily with a calculator.

A1 Find the length marked **?** in each of these diagrams.

(a)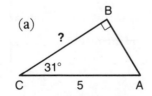

(b)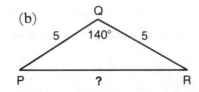

The answers to question A1 are as follows.

(a)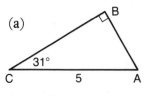

BC = **5 cos 31°**

(b)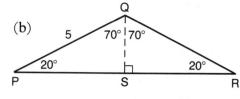

PS = **5 cos 20°** or **5 sin 70°**

So PR = **10 cos 20°** or **10 sin 70°**

Notice the two alternative answers to part (b). They arise because you can think of PS as adjacent to 20°, or as opposite 70°.

If two angles add up to 90°, the sine of one is the cosine of the other. (So an alternative answer to part (a) is BC = 5 sin 59°.)

A2 Find the lengths marked **?** in each of these diagrams.

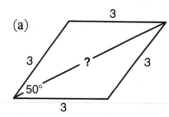

A3 ABCD is a rhombus. The diagonal AC is of length 10 units. Find the length of the side AB if angle ABC is

(a) 40°   (b) 60°   (c) 140°   (d) 120°

A4 Find the area of each of these shapes.

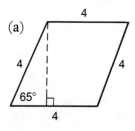

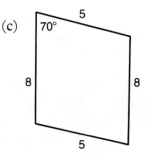

ABCDE is a regular pentagon with sides of length 10 units.

The vertices of the pentagon are on a circle. (We say the pentagon is **inscribed** in the circle.)

O is the centre of the circle.
M is the midpoint of AE.

Make your own copy of the diagram.

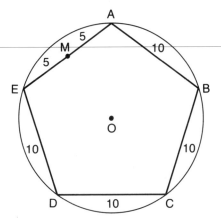

(a) Work out the angles BOA, OBA and BAC.

(b) Find the length of the diagonal AC.

(c) Work out the angles AOE, ACE and ACM.

(d) Find the length of CM.

(e) Work out the angle AOM.

(f) Find the length of AO.

(g) N is the midpoint of AC. Find the length of ON.

A regular pentagon ABCDE has sides of length 1 unit.

The five diagonals enclose a smaller regular pentagon VWXYZ.

Find the length of a side of this smaller pentagon.

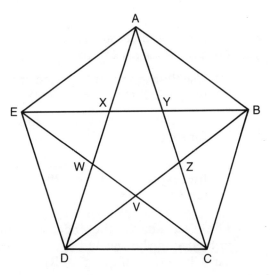

B The sine, cosine and tangent of 45°, 60°, 30°

If *d* is the length of a diagonal of a square of side 1 unit, then

$$d^2 = 1^2 + 1^2 = 2.$$

So $d = \sqrt{2}$.

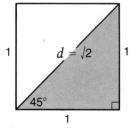

From the shaded right-angled triangle, we have

$\sqrt{2} \sin 45° = 1$ $\quad\quad$ $\sqrt{2} \cos 45° = 1$ $\quad\quad$ $1 \tan 45° = 1$

From which we get

$$\sin 45° = \frac{1}{\sqrt{2}} \quad\quad \cos 45° = \frac{1}{\sqrt{2}} \quad\quad \tan 45° = 1$$

We get an alternative form for sin 45° and cos 45° by multiplying 'top and bottom' by $\sqrt{2}$.

$$\sin 45° = \cos 45° = \frac{\sqrt{2}}{2}$$

(To 8 decimal places, $\sqrt{2}$ is 1·41421356, so sin 45° to 8 decimal places is 0·70710678.)

B1 ABC is an equilateral triangle whose sides are of length 2 units.

(a) Use Pythagoras' rule to find the height BD. (No calculators!)

(b) Use triangle ABD to find expressions for sin 60°, cos 60° and tan 60°.

(c) Use the fact that angle ABD is 30° to find expressions for sin 30°, cos 30° and tan 30°.

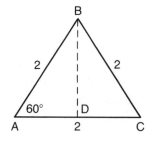

The exact values of the sine, cosine and tangent of 60° and 30° are printed at the bottom of page 55. Check your answers to parts (b) and (c) of question B1 before you continue.

Use the exact values of sin 45°, sin 60°, etc. in the answers to this question.

(a) The sides of a rectangular hexagon ABCDEF are each 4 units long. Find the length of the diagonal AC.

(b) PQRSTU is a regular hexagon. The distance between the parallel sides PQ and TS is 10 units. Calculate the length of each side of the hexagon.

(c) ABCDEFGH is a regular octagon whose sides are each 2 units long. Find the length of the diagonal AD.

Regular polygons inscribed in a circle

If you want to draw a regular polygon really accurately, the best way is to start with a fairly large circle and draw lines radiating out from the centre at equal angles.

The points on the circle where these lines meet it will be the vertices of a regular polygon.

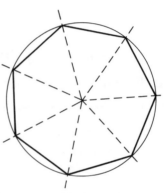

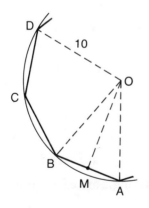

C1 This diagram shows part of a regular 9-sided polygon inscribed in a circle whose centre is at O.

The radius of the circle is 10 units. M is the midpoint of the side AB.

(a) Explain why AM = 10 sin 20°, and write down the length AB in terms of sin 20°.

(b) Find expressions for AC and AD in terms of the sines of certain angles.

---

sin 60° = cos 30° = $\frac{\sqrt{3}}{2}$;   cos 60° = sin 30° = $\frac{1}{2}$;   tan 60° = $\sqrt{3}$;   tan 30° = $\frac{1}{\sqrt{3}} = \frac{\sqrt{3}}{3}$.

Here is the working for finding AD in question C1.

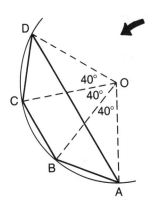

The angles at the centre are each $\frac{360°}{9} = 40°$.

So angle AOD is 120°.

The triangle AOD can be split into two right-angled triangles.

AN = 10 sin 60°

So AD = 2AN = **20 sin 60°**
(or **10√3**)

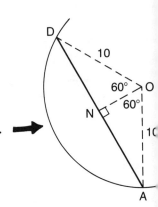

C2 A regular pentagon is inscribed in a circle of radius 8 units.

(a) Find the length of each side.

(b) Find the length of each diagonal.

(c) Write down expressions for the side and diagonal when the radius of the circle is (i) 20 units (ii) 13 units (ii) r units

In questions C1 and C2, you were given the radius of the circle and asked to find the length of a side of the regular polygon.
In practice, the problem is usually the other way round: what size of circle to draw to get a polygon whose sides will be a given length.

The circle itself is called the **circumcircle** of the regular polygon. Its radius is called the **circumradius** of the polygon.

C3 (a) An equilateral triangle of side 2 units is inscribed in a circle. Find the radius of the circle (the circumradius of the triangle).

(b) Find the circumradius when the sides of the triangle are each 5 units.

(c) Find the circumradius when the sides of the triangle are each a units.

C4 Find the circumradius of a square of side a units.

C5 Find the circumradius of a regular pentagon of side 8 units.

Find the circumradius of (a) a regular pentagon of side a units

(b) a regular pentagon of diagonal d units

ABCDEFGH is a regular octagon. Each side is 6 units long.

(a) Find the circumradius of the octagon.

(b) Find the lengths of the diagonals AC, AD and AE.

Diagonals of regular polyhedra

P and Q are two vertices of a cube whose edges are each of length a units.

(a) How many different possible values are there for the distance PQ?

(b) What are the possible values for PQ?

Repeat question D1 for a regular octahedron of edge 2 units.

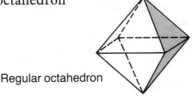

Regular octahedron

Have a good go at this problem before you turn over.

Repeat question D1 for a regular icosahedron of edge 2 units.

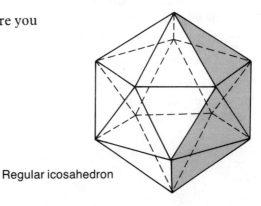

Regular icosahedron

You may have found question D3 a bit hard. But it is not so difficult if you break it down into stages.

You will find it easier to see what to do if you have a model of a regular icosahedron to look at!

Each edge of the icosahedron is 2 units long. So if P and Q are adjacent vertices, the distance PQ must be 2 units. The difficulties arise, of course, when P and Q are not adjacent.

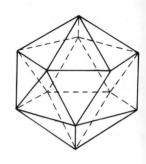

In that case the shortest path from P to Q **going along edges** will be either two edges long or three edges long.

D4 Suppose P an Q are 'two edges apart', as in the diagram on the right.

(a) How many vertices are joined to both P and Q?

(b) Let V be a vertex which is joined to P and to Q. Look at the three-dimensional shape formed by V and the five vertices joined to it. They form a pyramid. What shape is its base? So what is the length of PQ?

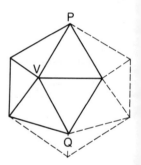

D5 Now suppose that P and Q are 'three edges apart'.

(a) Does it matter which pair you choose, or is the distance PQ the same for every pair of vertices which are 'three edges apart'?

Imagine the icosahedron inscribed inside a sphere.

Think of P as the 'north pole' and Q as the 'south pole' of the sphere.

PQ is a diameter of the sphere, so it is enough to find the radius r, and then double it.

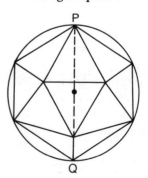

(Continued on next page.)

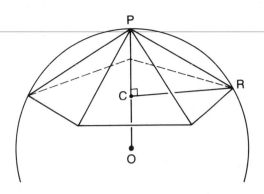

The vertex P and its five neighbours form a pyramid whose base is a regular pentagon.

Let O be the centre of the sphere, and R a vertex which is a neighbour of P.

Let the radius OP cut the base of the pyramid at C, which is the centre of the regular pentagon.

(b) Find CR. (No calculators!)

(c) Find CP.

(d) Hence express OC in terms of r.

(e) Use triangle OCR to find r.

(f) Hence find PQ. (See previous diagram.)

Here is another way to tackle the problem, once you have found CP.

Draw a line from O at right-angles to PR. Let it meet PR at S.

Explain why triangles OSP and RCP are similar.

Use this fact to find OP and hence PQ.

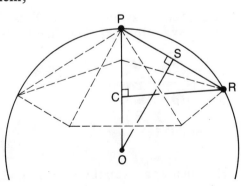

Problems and investigations (3)

1 Fault lines

You have rectangular tiles, each 1 unit by 2 units. You arrange them to make larger rectangles.

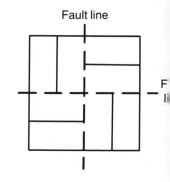

Sometimes you get 'fault lines' which run right across the larger rectangle from one side to the opposite side.

(a) What is the smallest rectangle that can be tiled by 2 by 1 tiles without producing any fault lines? (Other than a 2 by 1 rectangle itself!)

(b) What is the smallest square?

2 X-ray eggs

An ordinary egg box holds 6 eggs when full.

Eight boxes are stacked like this, but there are some empty spaces in the boxes.

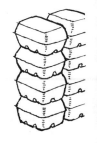

Here is an X-ray top view, an X-ray front view, and an X-ray side view (taken from the right-hand side).

Plan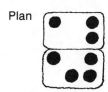

Front view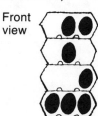

Right-hand side view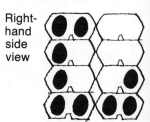

How many eggs can there be altogether in the boxes?

3 Shunting trucks

This diagram shows a train of goods trucks. They are in the wrong order. The numbers show where each truck ought to be in the train. ('1' indicates which truck should be first, and so on.)

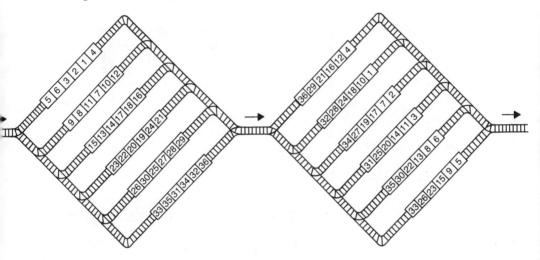

The trucks are first shunted on to this set of parallel tracks, . . .   then on to this set, . . .

. . . and they finally leave in the correct order.

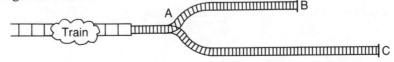

(a) Explain how the system works.

(b) Investigate other ways of re-ordering trains.

(c) Explain how a train may be re-ordered in any way on the layout below, provided that there is room for the whole train in the pair of sidings AB and AC.

4 Twelve equal circles touch each other round the edge of a circle of radius 10 cm.

Calculate the radius of each of the twelve circles.

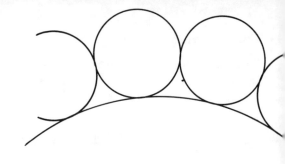

5 Printing cards

A pack of 16 cards is made by folding a large sheet of card in half, then in half again, then again, then again, like this.

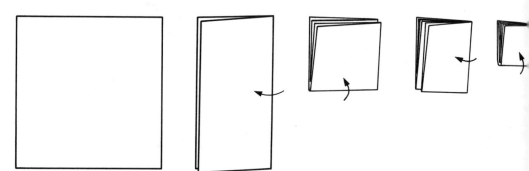

After this, the edges are cut to get the 16 cards.

The original sheet has to be printed so that the pack finally comes out numbered from 1 to 16, like this.

How should the numbers be printed on the original sheet?
Solve this problem without any folded paper!

Suggestions for solving the 'broken window puzzle' on page 50

Here are two ways you could try to solve the puzzle. (There are other ways besides these.)

One way is to take each pupil in turn and **assume** that he or she is the truth-teller.
Then you work out what the **consequences** would be of that person being the truth-teller.

For example, suppose you first assume that Sandra is the truth-teller. If Sandra is telling the truth, then Paul must have broken the window. But if Paul broke the window, then Wendy also must be telling the truth when she says 'It wasn't me'.

So by assuming that Sandra is the truth-teller we have found someone else who must also be telling the truth. But the puzzle says that only **one** person is telling the truth. So our assumption that Sandra is telling the truth leads to a consequence which does not fit all the facts given in the puzzle. We must therefore move on to each of the other four in turn and see what follows from assuming that he or she is telling the truth.

A different approach to the problem is to take each pupil in turn and assume for the moment that he or she is the person who broke the window.

For example, you could assume that Sandra broke the window. You then go on to work out who would be telling the truth and who would be lying, and see whether the consequences fit the facts given in the puzzle.

Both of these methods are called 'methods of elimination', because they involve trying all the possibilities one by one and eliminating (getting rid of) the ones that do not fit the facts given in the puzzle.

8 Powers

A Multiplying powers of the same number

a^4 means $a \times a \times a \times a$, and a^3 means $a \times a \times a$.
So $a^4 \times a^3 = a \times a \times a \times a \times a \times a \times a = a^7$.
Notice that the indices 4 and 3 are **added**: $a^4 \times a^3 = a^{4+3} = a^7$.

Of course, this is only true if we are multiplying powers of the same number. There is no simpler way of writing $a^4 b^3$, for example.
But $a^4 b^3 \times a^3 b^6$ can be simplified to $a^7 b^9$.

A1 Write each of these as a single power of a or x.

(a) $a^5 \times a^3$ (b) $x^2 \times x^3 \times x^4$ (c) $a^6 \times a \times a^2$ (d) $x^3 \times x^8 \times x^{20}$

A2 Simplify each of these expressions.

(a) $a^2 b \times ab^2$ (b) $pq^3 \times p^2 q^5$ (c) $x \times xy \times xy^2$ (d) $a^5 b^3 \times b^2 c^3 \times ac^2$

a^5 means $a \times a \times a \times a \times a$, and a^2 means $a \times a$.

So $\dfrac{a^5}{a^2} = \dfrac{a \times a \times a \times \cancel{a} \times \cancel{a}}{\cancel{a} \times \cancel{a}} = a \times a \times a = a^3$.

Notice that the indices are **subtracted**: $\dfrac{a^5}{a^2} = a^{5-2} = a^3$.

A3 Simplify each of these expressions.

(a) $\dfrac{a^8}{a^6}$ (b) $\dfrac{x^{10}}{x^7}$ (c) $\dfrac{a^4 b^9}{ab^3}$ (d) $\dfrac{x^{20} y^{30} z^{10}}{xyz}$ (e) $\dfrac{a^8 bc^5}{abc^3}$

If we apply the subtraction rule to $\dfrac{a^2}{a^5}$ we get a^{2-5}, or a^{-3}.

But $\dfrac{a^2}{a^5} = \dfrac{\cancel{a} \times \cancel{a}}{\cancel{a} \times \cancel{a} \times a \times a \times a} = \dfrac{1}{a^3}$. So a^{-3} has to be equal to $\dfrac{1}{a^3}$.

If we apply the subtraction rule to $\dfrac{a^3}{a^3}$, we get a^{3-3}, or a^0.

But $\dfrac{a^3}{a^3} = 1$. So a^0 has to be equal to 1, whatever the value of a.

From this we get another way of explaining why $\dfrac{1}{a^3}$ is equal to a^{-3}.

$$\dfrac{1}{a^3} = \dfrac{a^0}{a^3} = a^{0-3} = a^{-3}$$

4 Calculate these. Give the answers as fractions where appropriate.
(The first is done as an example.)

(a) $3^{-2} = \dfrac{1}{3^2} = \dfrac{1}{9}$ (b) 2^{-3} (c) 10^{-4} (d) 6^{-2} (e) 8^{-1} (f) $(\tfrac{1}{3})^{-2}$

5 Write each of these expressions as a single power of a.

(a) $\dfrac{1}{a^5}$ (b) $\dfrac{a^2}{a^6}$ (c) $a^{-5} \times a^{-2}$ (d) $a^{-5} \times a^2$ (e) $a^{-2} \times a^8$ (f) $\dfrac{a^3}{a^{-6}}$ (g) $\dfrac{a^{-4}}{a^6}$

The four 'rules of indices' which we have met so far can be summarised as follows.

$a^m \times a^n = a^{m+n}$ $\quad \dfrac{a^m}{a^n} = a^{m-n}$ $\quad a^0 = 1$ $\quad a^{-n} = \dfrac{1}{a^n}$

There is another rule, for simplifying **powers of powers**, for example $(a^4)^3$.

$$(a^4)^3 = a^4 \times a^4 \times a^4 = a^{12}$$

Notice that in this case the indices 4 and 3 are **multiplied**.

$$(a^4)^3 = a^{4 \times 3} = a^{12}$$

The general rule is: $(a^m)^n = a^{mn}$.

6 Write each of these as a single power of 2. Then calculate its value.
(Give answers as fractions where appropriate.)

(a) $(2^3)^2$ (b) $(2^3)^{-2}$ (c) $(2^{-1})^4$ (d) $(2^{-3})^{-2}$ (e) $(2^5)^2$ (f) $(2^{-2})^{-5}$

Calculating large powers of a number

Suppose we want to calculate 5^{10}. The obvious way to do it is this:

$5 \times 5 \times 5 \times 5 \times 5 \times 5 \times 5 \times 5 \times 5 \times 5.$

If the calculator has a squaring key, we can shorten the calculation. Here is one way to do it.

Enter 5 →[Square]→ 5^2 →[Square]→ 5^4 →[Square]→ 5^8 →[Multiply by 5^2]→ 5^{10}

A7 Here is another method of working out 5^{10}. One instruction is missing. What is the missing instruction?

Enter 5 →[Square]→[Square]→[...]→[Square]→ 5^{10}

A8 If we replace 5 by a, the first method above of working out a^{10} can be written as

$$((a^2)^2)^2 \times a^2.$$

Write out the second method in a similar way.

A9 Devise some different methods of working out a^{15} using the squaring operation and trying to shorten the calculation as much as you can. You may use the calculator's memory if you wish.

Use your methods to work out $(2 \cdot 5)^{15}$.

A10 The table below shows values of x^n for various values of x between 0 and 1, and for $n = 1, 2, 3, 4, 5, 6$ and 10.

Calculate the missing entries in the table, correct to 3 decimal places. (A dash indicates a value is less than $0 \cdot 001$ but not actually 0.)

x	0	0·2	0·4	0·6	0·8	0·9	0·95	1
x^2	0	0·040	0·160	0·360	0·640	0·810	0·903	1
x^3	0	0·008	0·064	0·216	0·512			1
x^4	0	0·0016	0·026	0·130	0·410			1
x^5	0	–	0·010	0·078	0·328			1
x^6	0	–	–	0·047	0·262			1
x^{10}	0	–	–	–	0·107			1

The graph of $x \to x^n$ for values of x between 0 and 1

The graphs of the functions $x \to x$, $x \to x^2$ and $x \to x^3$ for values of x from 0 to 1 are shown below.

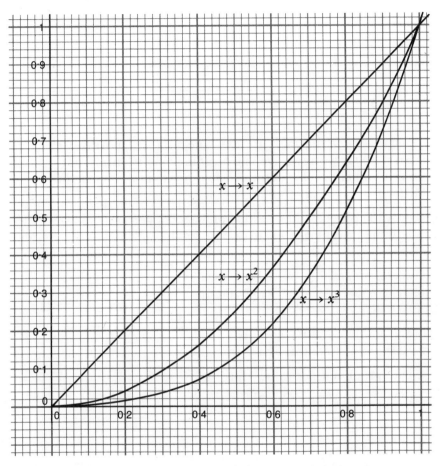

1 (a) Draw axes like those above. Use the table you made for question A10 to draw, as well as you can, the graphs of $x \to x^4$, $x \to x^5$, $x \to x^6$ and $x \to x^{10}$.

  (b) Draw a sketch of what you think the graph of $x \to x^{100}$ will look like, between $x = 0$ and $x = 1$.

  (c) Draw a sketch to show how the graphs of $x \to x^2$, $x \to x^3$ and $x \to x^4$ continue to the left of $x = 0$, for values of x from 0 down to $^-1$.

B Fractional indices

In the previous section, we looked at the graphs of $x \to x^2$, $x \to x^3$, etc.

In this section, we shall let x be the **index**, and look, for example, at the function $x \to 2^x$.

Here is a table of values for the function $x \to 2^x$.

x	$^-3$	$^-2$	$^-1$	0	1	2	3
2^x	$\frac{1}{8} = 0\cdot 125$	$\frac{1}{4} = 0\cdot 25$	$\frac{1}{2} = 0\cdot 5$	1	2	4	8

The values of x in this table are all whole numbers, positive or negative. So far we have given no meaning to 2^x when x is not a whole number. So, for example, we cannot put a value in the table for $x = \frac{1}{2}$ (or $0\cdot 5$).

One way to approach the question of what happens to 2^x between the whole-number values of x is to draw a graph.

B1 Draw axes on graph paper. Use the scales shown here (across from $^-3$ to 3 and up from 0 to 8).

Plot the points from the table above and draw a smooth curve through them.

Use your graph to find 'values' for

(a) $2^{0\cdot 5}$ (b) $2^{1\cdot 5}$ (c) $2^{2\cdot 5}$

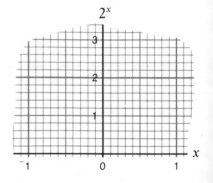

B2 So far we have given no meaning to points on the graph between the whole-number values of x.

But from the graph, when x is $0\cdot 5$, it appears that $2^{0\cdot 5}$ is about $1\cdot 4$.

Why? Think about this before you read on. (What number do you know which is approximately $1\cdot 4$?)

Think what happens if we multiply $2^{0.5}$ by itself, and use the rules of indices

$$2^{0.5} \times 2^{0.5} = 2^{0.5 + 0.5} = 2^1 = 2$$

So when we square $2^{0.5}$, we get 2. It follows that $2^{0.5}$, or $2^{\frac{1}{2}}$, is $\sqrt{2}$, and to 3 decimal places $\sqrt{2}$ is 1·414.

From the graph it should appear that $2^{1.5}$ is about 2·8.

What number is $2^{1.5}$ the square root of? Find $2^{1.5}$ to 5 d.p.

If we know the value of $2^{0.5}$, we can find the value of $2^{1.5}$ by using the rules of indices, like this.

$$2^{1.5} = 2^1 \times 2^{0.5}$$

Given that $2^{0.5} = 1.414$ to 3 d.p., use this method to find approximate values for   (a) $2^{2.5}$ (b) $2^{3.5}$

We have seen that $2^{0.5}$, or $2^{\frac{1}{2}}$, is equal to $\sqrt{2}$, because $2^{\frac{1}{2}} \times 2^{\frac{1}{2}} = 2^1 = 2$. We can use a similar method to give a meaning to $2^{\frac{1}{3}}$.

From the fact that $2^{\frac{1}{3}} \times 2^{\frac{1}{3}} \times 2^{\frac{1}{3}} = 2^1 = 2$, it follows that $2^{\frac{1}{3}}$ is the **cube root** of 2.

The cube root of 2 is the number which, when it is cubed, gives 2.

The symbol for cube root is $\sqrt[3]{\ }$.   So $2^{\frac{1}{3}} = \sqrt[3]{2}$

$\sqrt[3]{2}$ can be calculated, to as many decimal places as we like, by the decimal search method.

$1.2^3 = 1.728$, so 1·2 is too small; $1.3^3 = 2.197$, so 1·3 is too big; . . .

Continue this decimal search, and find the value of $\sqrt[3]{2}$ to 2 d.p.

Use your answer to question B5 to find an approximate value for each of these. Check from the graph of $x \to 2^x$, where possible.
(a) $2^{\frac{2}{3}}$ (b) $2^{1\frac{1}{3}}$ (c) $2^{1\frac{2}{3}}$ (d) $2^{4\frac{1}{3}}$

What meaning should be given to $2^{\frac{1}{4}}$? Explain why, and describe how the value of $2^{\frac{1}{4}}$ could be calculated to a given number of decimal places.

The method used on the previous page to give meaning to $2^{0.5}$, $2^{1.5}$, etc. can be extended to give meanings to other fractional powers, including powers of numbers other than 2.

For example, suppose we want to give a meaning to $3^{\frac{1}{5}}$ (or $3^{0.2}$). We multiply $3^{\frac{1}{5}}$ by itself until we get a whole-number index.

$$\underbrace{3^{\frac{1}{5}} \times 3^{\frac{1}{5}} \times 3^{\frac{1}{5}} \times 3^{\frac{1}{5}} \times 3^{\frac{1}{5}}}_{(3^{\frac{1}{5}})^5} = 3^1 = 3$$

So $3^{\frac{1}{5}}$ is the number which, when taken to the power 5, gives 3. We call this number the **fifth root** of 3, and write it $\sqrt[5]{3}$.

As before, we can calculate it to any number of decimal places, by the decimal search method.

$1 \cdot 2^5 = 2 \cdot 488\,32$, so $1 \cdot 2$ is too small; $\quad 1 \cdot 3^5 = 3 \cdot 712\,93$, so $1 \cdot 3$ is too big;

and so on. To three decimal places, $\sqrt[5]{3}$ is $1 \cdot 246$.

B8 Given that $\sqrt[5]{3}$ is approximately $1 \cdot 246$, calculate approximate values for
(a) $3^{\frac{2}{5}}$ (b) $3^{\frac{3}{5}}$ (c) $3^{0.8}$ (d) $3^{1.8}$ (e) $3^{2.6}$

Powers on a calculator

Many scientific calculators have a key which makes it possible to calculate powers of a number directly, including powers where the index is fractional.

This key is usually marked $\boxed{y^x}$ or $\boxed{x^y}$ and the usual key sequence for working out 2^3, say, is

$$\boxed{2}\;\boxed{y^x}\;\boxed{3}\;\boxed{=}$$

B9 Use the 'power' key to calculate $16^{0.5}$. Is the result what you should have expected?.

B10 Explain how to use the power key to find (a) $\sqrt{7}$ (b) $\sqrt[3]{7}$ (c) $\sqrt[4]{7}$ (d) $\sqrt[5]{7}$

C Exponential growth

Suppose a population of organisms doubles during every hour.
If the population is 5 million to start with, then t hours from the start it will be

$$5 \text{ million} \times \underbrace{2 \times 2 \times 2 \times \ldots \times 2}_{t \text{ times}} = 5 \times 2^t \text{ million}.$$

Here we have assumed that t is a whole number, but it is not necessary to assume this.
For example, the population 1·5 hours from the start is $5 \times 2^{1 \cdot 5}$ million, which to 3 significant figures is 14·1 million.

The graph of the population as a function of t looks like this.

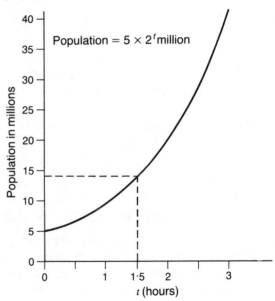

C1 (a) Calculate the population (to 3 s.f.) when $t = 1 \cdot 8$.

(b) Calculate the population when $t = 0 \cdot 8$.

(c) Explain why the answer to part (b) is half the answer to (a).

By using the power key we can calculate the population for any value of t. But suppose the problem is the other way round: for example, when will the population reach 25 million? We need to find the value of t for which

$$5 \times 2^t = 25,$$
$$\text{and so} \quad 2^t = 5.$$

Explain how you can find this value of t to 2 decimal places.

D Logarithmic scales

This scale is an ordinary **uniform** scale.

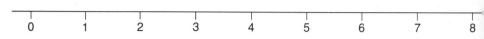

On this scale, intervals of equal length correspond to equal **additions**. For example, the interval from 2 to 5 is equal in length to the interval from 4 to 7, and both correspond to the addition +3.

A **logarithmic** scale is one on which intervals of equal length correspond to equal **multiplications**. Here is an example.

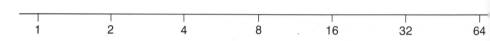

The interval from 2 to 8, for example, is equal in length on the scale to the interval from 16 to 64, and both correspond to the multiplication ×4.

D1 Show how the logarithmic scale above continues to the left of 1. Why can there be no mark for 0 on the scale?

An example of a logarithmic scale occurs in music. When a piano string vibrates, it does so with a certain frequency. Frequency is measured in **hertz**, 1 Hz being 1 vibration per second.

Low notes have low frequencies and high notes have high frequencies. The frequency of the note 'A above middle C' has been fixed by international agreement at 440 Hz. (This is the note which is sounded before an orchestra plays, to allow the players to tune their instruments.)

The frequency doubles as you go up an octave (eight white notes on a piano) so the scale of frequencies looks like this.

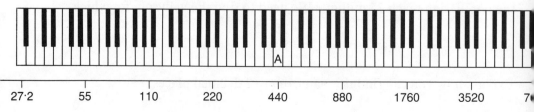

Logarithmic scales are often used to show a very wide range of numbers. The scale below shows the wavelengths of various kinds of electromagnetic radiation.

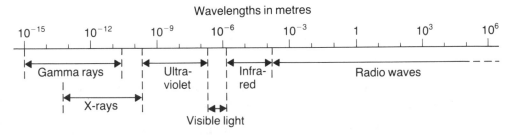

Each division on this scale corresponds to multiplication by 10.

Constructing a logarithmic scale

Look again at the logarithmic scale halfway down the opposite page. Whereabouts on the scale should we mark the number 3? The first guess might be to mark 3 halfway between 2 and 4, like this.

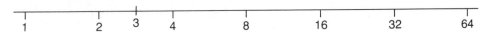

Now we have an interval from 1 to 3, which corresponds to multiplication by 3. Because of the principle underlying the logarithmic scale, every interval which is the same length as this one will also correspond to multiplication by 3.

But that means the interval from 3 to 8 should also correspond to multiplication by 3, which it obviously doesn't.
So we can't put 3 halfway between 2 and 4. It must be more than halfway, so that 9 will be beyond 8, something like this.

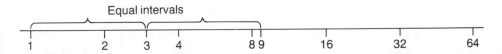

But how can we find **exactly** where to mark 3? Think about this yourself before you turn over.

Let us use the distance from the '1' mark to the '2' mark as our unit for measuring distances along the scale.

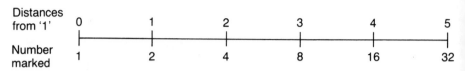

If we let x stand for the distance along the scale (starting from the 1 mark), then the number marked at distance x is 2^x.

We want to find where to mark the number 3. So, in other words, we want to find the value of x for which $2^x = 3$.

We shall see shortly how we can solve this problem using a calculator. Here we will see how it can be done by using the graph of $x \to 2^x$.

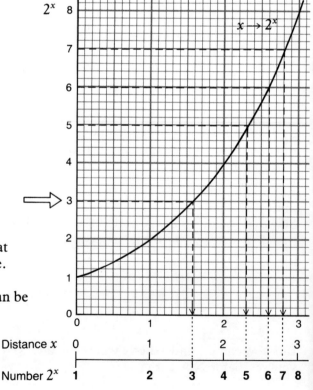

We find the value of x for which $2^x = 3$.
It is approximately 1·6.

The mark for '3' is placed at distance 1·6 along the scale.

The marks for 5, 6 and 7 can be made in a similar way.

The value of x for which $2^x = 3$ can also be found by using a calculator. The next question shows how.

2   It is obvious that x lies between 1 and 2, because $2^1 = 2$ and $2^2 = 4$.

Try values of x between 1 and 2, and use the power key to find 2^x. Continue the decimal search to find the value of x to 2 decimal places.

3   Solve the equation $2^x = 7$ in a similar way.

The slide rule

The slide rule is a calculating device for doing multiplication and division and certain other types of calculation. Slide rules were in common use before electronic calculators became available.

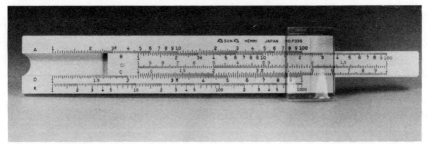

The basic component of a slide rule is a pair of identical logarithmic scales which slide alongside one another. In the diagram below, the two scales are set to do $1·7 \times 2·6$ (or $1·7 \times$ any other number). The answers obtained from a slide rule are only approximate.

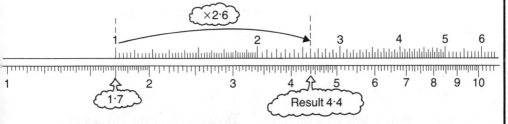

Notice how the principle of the logarithmic scale is used here: the interval from 1 to $2·6$ corresponds to multiplication by $2·6$.

E Logarithms

Here again is a table of values of 2^x for whole-number values of x from 0 to 6.

x	0	1	2	3	4	5	6
2^x	1	2	4	8	16	32	64

Look at the value of 2^6, which is 64.

The index, 6, is called the **logarithm to base 2** of 64.

The symbol for 'logarithm to base 2' is $\log_2$, so we write $\log_2 64 = 6$.

From the table we see that, for example, $\log_2 16 = 4$,
$$\log_2 32 = 5, \text{ etc.}$$

The simplest way to define the log-to-base-2 of a number N is this:

$\log_2 N$ is the index x for which $2^x = N$.

Any statement about a power of 2 can be re-written as a statement about a logarithm to base 2, and vice versa.

For example, the statement $2^8 = 256$ can be re-written as $\log_2 256 = 8$.

E1 (a) Calculate 2^7 and write a corresponding statement containing $\log_2$.

(b) Do the same for 2^{10} and for 2^{15}.

E2 (a) Use the power key to calculate $2^{3 \cdot 6}$ to 3 decimal places.

Now write down a corresponding statement containing $\log_2$.

(b) Repeat for (i) $2^{0 \cdot 6}$ (ii) $2^{5 \cdot 73}$ (iii) $2^{0 \cdot 584}$

E3 Re-write each of these statements in a form containing a power of 2.

(a) $\log_2 2048 = 11$ (b) $\log_2 2 \cdot 48 = 1 \cdot 31$ (c) $\log_2 1 \cdot 64 = 0 \cdot 71$

Check your statements on a calculator. (Do not expect the checks to work out exactly, because the numbers in the statements above have been rounded off to 2 d.p.)

4 (a) Re-write the statement $x = \log_2 80$ in power form.

(b) Use a decimal search to find the value of $\log_2 80$ to 1 decimal place.

5 (a) Explain why $\log_2 30$ must be between 4 and 5.

(b) Calculate $\log_2 30$ to 1 decimal place.

6 The graph of $x \to 2^x$ on page 74 can be used to find, approximately, the logs-to-base-2 of numbers.

(a) Explain how the graph can be used to find $\log_2 6$.

(b) Copy this table and use the graph to complete it.

Number N	1	2	3	4	5	6	7	8
$\log_2 N$								

(c) Draw a new graph, with the following axes:

across: N, from 0 to 8 (1 cm to 1 unit);
up: $\log_2 N$, from 0 to 3 (2 cm to 1 unit)

Plot the points from the table and draw a smooth curve through them.

(d) How is this second graph related to the graph of $x \to 2^x$?

(e) Draw a sketch to show how the second graph continues for values of N below 1.

For individual research

So far we have looked only at logarithms to base 2, but logarithms can be to any base. Logarithms to base 10 have been used frequently in the past.

The log-to-base-10 of a number can be defined like this:

$\log_{10} N$ is the index x for which $10^x = N$

So, for example, $\log_{10} 100 = 2$, because $10^2 = 100$,
$\log_{10} 1000 = 3$, because $10^3 = 1000$.

Find out how tables of logarithms to base 10 were used to shorten the work involved in calculations on paper, in the days before electronic calculators became available.

Problems and investigations (4)

1 **Diagonals of regular polygons**

   (a) The diagonals of a regular 7-sided polygon are of two different lengths. (One of each length is shown in this diagram.)

   How many diagonals are there altogether equal in length to a? How many are equal in length to b?

   (b) How many different lengths of diagonal are there in a regular polygon with n sides? How many diagonals are there of each length?

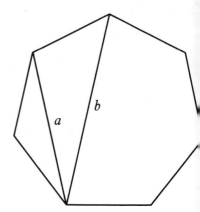

2 **Floating cuboids**

A solid cuboid 1 unit by 2 units by 3 units floats magically in space. What is the largest number of magically floating cuboids, each also 1 unit by 2 units by 3 units, which can be arranged to touch the first cuboid?

3 **The longest path**

   Find the longest path which

       starts at A and finishes at B.

       consists of straight lines going from one dot to another,

       visits every dot once and once only,

       does not cross itself.

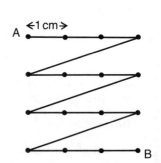

Calculate the length of the longest path.

(Needless to say, the path shown in the diagram is **not** the longest path!)

4 Success story

Microtome is a magazine for home computer owners. The editor knows that each year more people own home computers and she judges the success of *Microtome* by calculating what proportion of computer owners buy the magazine.

She has four regional sales managers. Each of these has to use advertising in his or her area to encourage as many computer owners as possible to buy the magazine.

At the end of the year the sales managers get together to see how successful they have been. Here are their results.

Region	Last year			This year		
	Number of computer owners	Number buying *Microtome*	Proportion buying *Microtome*	Number of computer owners	Number buying *Microtome*	Proportion buying *Microtome*
South-west	41 000	2200	5·4%	98 000	5900	6·0%
South-east	48 000	8300	17·3%	64 000	11 700	18·3%
Midlands	34 000	2600	7·6%	115 000	10 100	8·8%
North	40 000	8500	21·3%	41 000	10 100	24·6%

They are all very pleased. Not only has the number of *Microtome* buyers increased in every region, but in each region the proportion of computer owners buying the magazine has also gone up. (The North region manager is particularly pleased with his results.)

'Wait a moment,' says the editor. 'Let's see what has happened to the proportion of computer owners buying the magazine over the country as a whole.'

So they did. You do the same, like this:

(a) Find the total number of computer owners in all four regions last year, and the total number of them who bought *Microtome*. Calculate what percentage of computer owners bought the magazine last year.

(b) Calculate this year's percentage in a similar way.

(c) What do you think the editor's reaction would be? Check the regional percentages if you think they might be wrong.

9 Topics in solid geometry

A Sections

If you cut a cube by a plane
through the points A, B and C, . . .

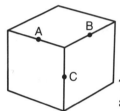

This is an example of
a plane **section** of a cube.

you get an equilateral triangle.

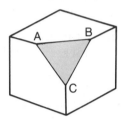

A1 *The diagrams for this question are on worksheet YE2–5.*
Draw the shape you would get from sections of the cube through
the marked points in each of these diagrams.

(a)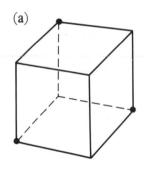

(b)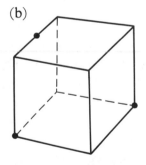

(c)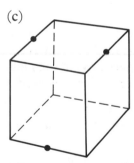

(d)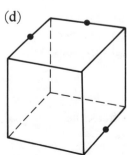

(e)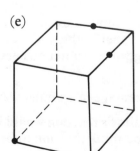

(f)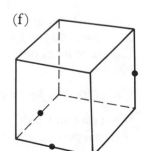

The diagrams for questions A2–A4 are on worksheet YE2–6.

A2 Can you cut a square-based pyramid by a single plane to get sections of the following shapes? If so, show how.

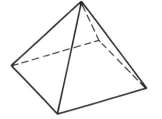

(a) an equilateral triangle

(b) a square

(c) an acute-angled isosceles triangle (all angles less than 90°)

(d) an obtuse-angled isosceles triangle (one angle greater than 90°)

(e) a right-angled isosceles triangle

(f) an isosceles trapezium

(g) a non-isosceles trapezium

(h) a kite

(i) a rhombus (other than a square)

A3 Can you find a plane section of a regular tetrahedron which is

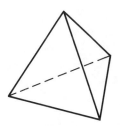

(a) a square

(b) a rectangle but not a square

A4 Can you find a plane section of a regular octahedron which is a regular hexagon?

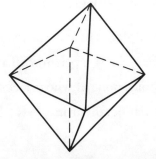

B Reflection symmetry in three dimensions

If you cut a chair in half, like this, . . .

. . . and put one half against a mirror, you see a whole chair.

The plane of the mirror is a **plane of reflection symmetry** of the chair.

B1 The plane p in this diagram is one plane of reflection symmetry of the hexagonal prism.

How many planes of symmetry does the prism have altogether?

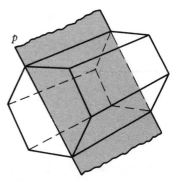

B2 The cross-section of a prism is an equilateral triangle.
How many planes of reflection symmetry does the prism have?
(There are more than three.)

B3 How many planes of symmetry do the following solids have?

(a) a cube   (b) a prism with a square cross-section (other than a cube)

(c) a cuboid, none of whose faces is a square   (d) a regular tetrahedron

(e) a regular octahedron   (f) a sphere   (g) a cone

C Rotation symmetry in three dimensions

In two dimensions, we have **centres** of rotation symmetry.

For example, the point C in the diagram on the right is a 6-fold centre of rotation symmetry.

If the design is rotated about the point C, there are 6 positions in which it will look the same as it did to start with (including the original position).

In three dimensions, we have lines, or **axes**, of rotation symmetry.

For example, the line a is a 3-fold axis of rotation symmetry of the equilateral triangular prism.

The line b is a 2-fold axis of rotation symmetry.

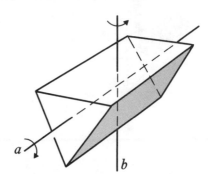

1 How many axes of rotation symmetry does this prism have altogether? How many of each type are there?

2 For each solid listed below, say how many 2-fold axes it has, how many 3-fold, etc. Draw sketches to show where the axes are.

   (a) a prism whose cross-section is a regular hexagon
   (b) a square-based pyramid with a vertex above the centre of the base
   (c) a regular tetrahedron
   (d) a cuboid, none of whose faces is a square
   (e) a prism with a square cross-section (other than a cube)

   Check your answers to this question before continuing.

3 How many axes of rotation symmetry does a cube have? How many 2-fold axes, how many 3-fold axes, etc.?

   This is not as easy as you might think. There are more than twelve axes altogether. You may find a model useful.

D Dihedral angles

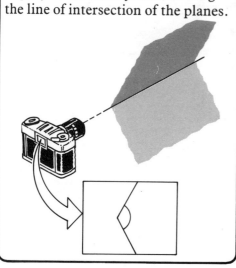

The **angle between two planes** is the angle you see when you look along the line of intersection of the planes.

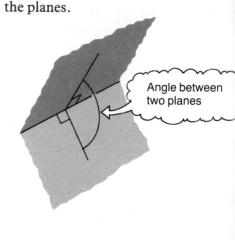

It is the angle between two lines, one each plane, which are drawn at right angles to the line of intersection of the planes.

Angle between two planes

D1 This diagram shows the roof of a house.

Calculate the angle between

(a) the planes ABC and ACDF

(b) the planes BEDC and ACDF

D2 The edges of a square-based pyramid are all of equal length. Calculate the angle between a triangular face and the square base.

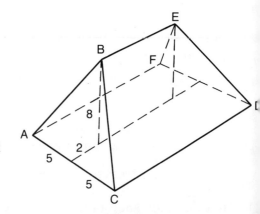

The angle between two adjacent faces of a polyhedron is called a **dihedral** angle.

(Dihedral = two-faced.)

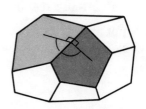

In a regular polyhedron, all the dihedral angles are equal.

3   What is the size of the dihedral angle of a cube?

4   Calculate the dihedral angle of a regular tetrahedron.

5   Is it possible to glue identical tetrahedra together as shown here, to make a closed 'ring'? (The shading shows the glued faces.)

  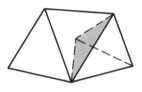

Explain the reason for your answer.

and so on

6   (a) Calculate the dihedral angle of a regular octahedron.

   (b) What do you notice about the dihedral angles of a regular octahedron and a regular tetrahedron?

   (c) What will you get if you glue a regular tetrahedron onto 'alternate' faces of a regular octahedron? (The faces of the two types of polyhedron are the same size.)

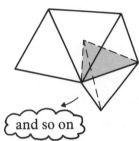

7   This solid is called a **square antiprism**. This one has edges of equal length.

   (a) How many different sizes of dihedral angle does the solid have?

   (b) Calculate the dihedral angles.

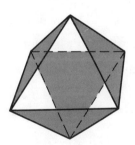

8   Calculate the dihedral angle of a regular icosahedron.

10 Logic puzzles (2)

There are a number of old puzzles about a traveller who lands on an island with two kinds of inhabitant, those who always tell the truth and those who always lie.

1   Suppose the traveller meets three islanders, A, B and C.
    She asks A whether he is a truth-teller but he mumbles and she cannot hear his answer.

    B says: 'A said that he is a liar.'

    C says: 'Don't believe B. He is lying.'

    (a) What is B, a truth-teller or a liar? (Think about A's answer.)

    (b) What is C?

2   Later on, the traveller meets three more islanders, E, F and G.
    She asks whether they are truth-tellers.

    E says: 'All three of us are truth-tellers.'

    F says: 'Don't listen to E. He is lying.'

    G says: 'F is telling the truth.'

    Who is a truth-teller and who is a liar?
    Give a reason for your answer.

3   The traveller meets another group of islanders, J, K and L.
    She asks J, 'How many of you are truth-tellers?' But she cannot hear J's reply.

    K says: 'J said only one of us is a truth-teller.'

    L says: 'K is lying.'

    Work out who is what.

    (If you get stuck, there is a hint at the bottom of the next page.)

Before she leaves the island, the traveller meets two more groups of islanders. Their replies are still more puzzling. See what you can work out from them.

One group consists of the islanders P, Q and R.

P says: 'All three of us are liars.'

Q says: 'Just one of us is a truth-teller.'

R says nothing.

(a) What can you say about P?
(b) How many truth-tellers can there be if Q's statement is false? Is this possible?
(c) If Q's statement is true, what does that make R? Give a reason.

The last group consists of islanders X, Y and Z.

X says: 'All three of us are liars.'

Y says: 'Just one of us is a liar.'

Z says nothing.

Can you work out who is what?

Hint for puzzle 3 on the previous page.
Can J and K both be telling the truth?

Problems and investigations (5)

The 'law of 70'

This is part of an article which appeared in *The Guardian* on 3 April 1984.

('GNP' stands for 'gross national product', which is a rough measure of how economically active a country is.)

Investigate the 'law of 70'.

ALTERNATIVES

Harford Thomas

THERE HAVE been moments recently when it seemed we might have to rehearse all over again the law of 70. This is the mental arithmetic way of converting percentage growth rates into doubling times by dividing 70 by the growth rate. So 2 per cent annual growth if sustained would double whatever it is — GNP, say, or population, to take two typical examples — in 35 years.

It explains why R. A. Butler, when he was Chancellor of the Exchequer in the early 1950s, forecast that the British standard of living could be doubled in 25 years. People at the time found that hard to believe, but he was not far out because the GNP growth rate was around 3 per cent during that time.

Correspondingly, the world population in the second h of this century has be doubling roughly every years, with an overall grow rate of around 2 per ce per. Politicians are am those who have yet to p gramme the facts of expor tially doubling redoubling into their thi ing.

Economic growth is expected objective of Ch cellors of the Exchequ During the 1960s Britain v falling behind the gro rates of some of the m successful European cc tries. If they could manag or 5 or even 6 per cent ec omic growth, why coul we? The question was rai in the Treasury, though know not with what answ The sensible answer wo have been that 5 per c growth would imply doubling of production a consumption in 14 years.

And the sensible re would have been, Yes, Ch cellor . . . but growth what, with what, and whom? As it was, e Britain's own quite moc dash for growth blew up 1972 and 1973, along w the rest of the industrial world. The post-1950 gro rates were unsustainable.

These reflections have b prompted by soce econo commentaries on the rec recovery of the UK grow rate which toy with the i of perhaps 4 per cent gro — and that means doubl up in 17 years or th abouts. Of what with and for whom?

1 Simulation

Pseudo-random sequences

Computers are frequently used to do the job which random devices such as dice and coins do. A computer called ERNIE (Electronic Random Number Indicator Equipment) is used to 'pick out' winning premium bond numbers.

Many home computers, and some calculators, will produce 'random sequences', usually made up of the digits 0 to 9. You can think of such a machine as 'pretending' to behave like a fair 10-sided dice. It is possible to use tests similar to those described in chapter 5 to see whether the sequence it produces is sufficiently 'dice-like'.

An early idea for a 'random number generator' which could be programmed into a computer was the 'middle-square' method. It works as follows:

> Start with a four-figure number, e.g. 6593, and square it: 43467649. Remove the last two digits and the first two, leaving the 'inside four': 4676. Square again and remove digits as before; and so on.

So we get: $6593^2 = 43\underline{4676}49$; $4676^2 = 21\underline{8649}76$; $8649^2 = 74\underline{8052}01$; . . .

The numbers we obtain, 4676, 8649, 8052, etc., are not really random. They can't be, because we can predict by calculation what the next one will be! But the sequence **appears** to be random, at least for a time, and this may be sufficient for practical purposes. The sequence is called a **pseudo-random sequence**.

Unfortunately the middle-square method has a serious weakness. It tends to generate only a few numbers before getting stuck in a rut.

Calculate the first ten numbers of the middle-square sequence starting with   (a) 4416   (b) 6100

Because of this weakness in the middle-square method, most computers and calculators use other methods to generate pseudo-random numbers.

A method which is sometimes used is to begin with a 'seed' – a random starting value – and generate a sequence by an iterative method such as this:

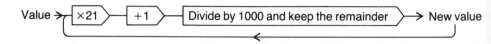

For example, if the seed value is 135, the sequence starts like this.

Whatever the seed value, this rule will produce all the numbers between 0 and 999, with each number appearing once only. Then it will reach the seed value again and the sequence will repeat itself.

So once a particular three-figure number comes up, then it will not repeat until 1000 numbers later. Obviously this is not the behaviour we expect from a proper random device, but the sequence may be 'random enough' for practical purposes.

There are problems, though. Suppose you wanted to use this sequence to imitate the results of tossing a coin. You decide to look at each three-digit number in turn, and if the number is odd it will stand for a head and if it is even, a tail.

A2 Look down the sequence on the right. What will happen if the numbers are used to represent heads and tails in the way suggested above?

A3 Look down the middle digits of the numbers in the sequence. Write about what you notice.

Although there is an obvious pattern in the right-hand digits and a less obvious pattern in the middle ones, the left-hand digits do not suffer from this defect. Most rules of the type used here produce sequences with the same tendency: the 'less significant' figures (those towards the right) show more regularity than the 'more significant' figures (towards the left). So where rules of this kind are used, they are usually designed to produce numbers with more digits than are needed, and then the digits towards the right are 'chopped off' and only those towards the left are displayed.

135
836
557
698
659
840
641
462
703
764
045
946
867
208
369
750
751
772
213
474
955
056
177
718
079
660
861
082
723
184
865
166
487
228
789
570
971
392
233
894
775
276
797
738
499
480
⋮

Using random numbers for sampling

There are other uses for random numbers besides imitating dice and coins.

Suppose a medical researcher wants to find out about the condition of children's teeth in a town. She visits the local school, which has 894 pupils. She will not have time to examine all of them, so she decides to choose a sample of 50 children, hoping that they will be representative of the dental health of the children as a whole.

If she goes into each classroom, looks around and just chooses a few children, she could be accused later of **bias**. If her research shows that the children's teeth are in a poor state, people might say that this was because she deliberately chose children who looked unhealthy.

One way to avoid this criticism is to give every pupil a different number, then to get 50 random numbers from a random number generator and examine the 50 children with these numbers. In that way, every child in the school has an equal chance of being chosen for the sample, not just the unhealthy-looking ones.

Simulating games

You need a calculator with a random number key, or a printed table of random numbers.

Here are the rules of a simple game for two players.

> One player is 'heads' and the other is 'tails'.
> They start with two matches each.
> A coin is tossed. If it lands head, the heads player takes one of the tails player's matches. If it lands tail, the tails player takes one of the heads player's matches.
> The game ends when one player is 'broke', that is, has no matches left.

If the coin is fair, the players have an equal chance of winning. But there are other things about the game that are less obvious. For example, how many throws, on average, does the game go on for? Or, if the players start with three matches each, will the game go on for longer? How much longer?

We can explore these questions by using random digits instead of a coin, and **simulating** the game. Instead of heads and tails we will call the imaginary players 'odd' and 'even'. If an odd random digit comes up, the odd player takes a match from the even player, and vice versa.

Here are the results of four 'games' simulated in this way.

Random digit	'Even' player	'Odd' player		Random digit	'Even' player	'Odd' player
	11	11	← Start of a game		11	11
0	111	1		6	111	1
1	11	11		2	1111	
5	1	111				
7		1111	← Game ends		11	11
				3	1	111
	11	11	← New game	6	11	11
1	1	111		0	111	1
6	11	11		7	11	11
9	1	111		3	1	111
7		1111	← Game ends	5		1111

B1 (a) Simulate a few more games using random digits. To save time you need only record one player's matches. When the number reaches 0 or 4, the game ends.

(b) Calculate the average length (average number of 'throws') of the games you have simulated.

B2 Simulate some more match games but this time starting with three matches each. Comment on how this affects the length of the game.

Many other questions can be answered by simulation. For example:

If you start with 3 matches each, what is the likelihood of a really long game, say of 30 throws?

To answer a question such as this, a large number of simulations of the game are needed. Fortunately this is easy on a computer.

A simulation of a fairground game

The fairground machine shown on the right works like this:

You put 5p in.
The pointer rotates and stops at a number.
If it stops at 1, it pays 1p; if at 2, it pays 2p; etc.

The machine has been tested and all ten numbers come up with similar frequencies in the long run. So a random number generator can be used to simulate the behaviour of the machine.

Suppose you have 6p before you start playing on the machine.
You put in 5p for your first spin, leaving you with 1p.
So long as you get at least 4p back, you will have enough for another spin.
But if at any stage you have less than 5p after a spin, you will be 'broke' and unable to play again.

Suppose the first three numbers are 7, 3, 1. The progress of the game can be shown like this:

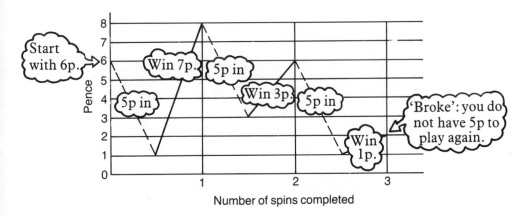

3 Use random numbers to simulate playing on the machine, starting with 6p, and continuing until you can no longer play. Do this a few times and see how many spins you get each time.

You perhaps discovered for yourself that you can sometimes be 'broke' (have less than 5p left) after only a few spins, but occasionally your trial will last for very many spins. (The word 'trial' is used here to mean a series of spins in which you start with 6p and end up 'broke'.)

To get an idea of how likely it is that a trial will last for 1 spin, 2 spins, 3 spins, etc., a computer can be programmed to simulate 1000 trials and record how many of them lasted for only 1 spin, how many for 2 spins, etc.

This bar chart has been drawn from the results of 1000 simulated trials, starting each time with 6p.

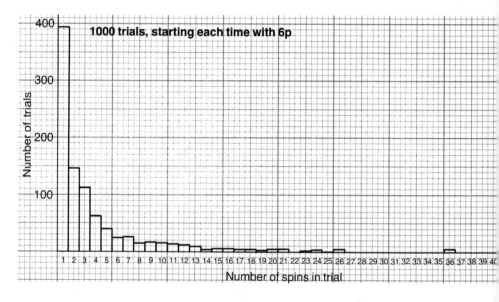

The shape of the bar chart confirms that the number of spins in a trial is most likely to be small, but it can just occasionally be very large.

If we were to start with more than 6p, then we would expect that on the whole trials would last longer before we went 'broke'.

94

This chart has been drawn from the results of another computer simulation of the game, but this time each of the 1000 trials began with 9p.

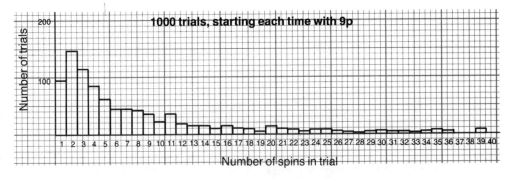

So with a bigger **reserve** to start with, trials tend to last longer. In the first bar chart, nearly 400 out of the 1000 trials (40%) lasted for only 1 spin. In the second chart, about 50% of the trials lasted 6 spins or more and about 10% lasted 32 spins or more. (Some of them are off the end of the chart!)

The fairground machine itself is biassed against the player. This is because the mean amount won per game is $\dfrac{0 + 1 + 2 + \ldots + 9}{10} = 4\cdot 5\text{p}$,

which is less than what it costs to play a game. It can be shown that a player is bound to end up 'broke' if he or she continues to play.

There is a listing for the computer program for this simulation in the teacher's guide. It will work with whatever starting amount (reserve) you give it.

C Stock control

Suppose a warehouse receives regular deliveries of goods from a factory, but that demands for goods to be sent out to customers are irregular. The manager of the warehouse wants to avoid running out of stock, because otherwise customers will go elsewhere.

This kind of problem arises frequently in business. To get some idea of how the problem may be tackled, we shall look at an imaginary, much simplified, example.

The Electronic Widget Company has a warehouse in which widgets are stored in truckloads. Customers order widgets in truckloads.

The manager has kept a record of the quantity of widgets sent out to customers in each month for the past 100 months. The number of times 1 truckload, 2 truckloads, etc. were sent out are given below.

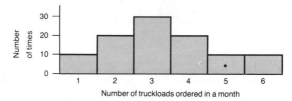

We can convert these figures into probabilities and say that the probability of one truckload being sent out in a month is $\frac{10}{100} = \frac{1}{10}$, the probability of two truckloads being sent out is $\frac{20}{100} = \frac{2}{10}$, etc.

To simulate the quantities sent out to customers we need a device which produces the numbers 1, 2, 3, 4, 5 and 6 not with equal probabilities but with the probabilities $\frac{1}{10}, \frac{2}{10}, \frac{3}{10}, \frac{2}{10}, \frac{1}{10}$ and $\frac{1}{10}$.

One such device is illustrated here.

Sequences produced by this device are called **non-uniform** random sequences, because we do not expect to get equal frequencies of each of the digits in a long sequence.

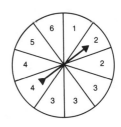

Calculators are programmed to give uniform random sequences made up of the digits 0 to 9. We can convert such a sequence into the kind of non-uniform random sequence we want here by this method.

When this digit comes up ..	0	1	2	3	4	5	6	7	8	9
. . . call it this	1	2	2	3	3	3	4	4	5	6

So, for example, 3 5 1 0 1 8 8 4 7 4 5 2 2 9 ...
becomes   3 3 2 1 2 5 5 3 4 3 3 2 2 6 ...

We are now in a position to simulate the flow of goods into and out of the warehouse, using an ordinary random number generator.

We will suppose that the warehouse operates in periods of six months. At the start of a six-month period, the manager can have as many truckloads in the warehouse as he likes. Then he receives deliveries of 3 truckloads each at the end of 1 month, 2 months, 3 months, 4 months and 5 months. At the end of 6 months he can again have what he likes, to start the next period.

We generate six random numbers, say   0   8   2   1   6   5,
and convert them to quantities sent out: 1   5   2   2   4   3.

The rises and falls of the stock level in the warehouse, measured from the starting level, are shown in the diagram below.

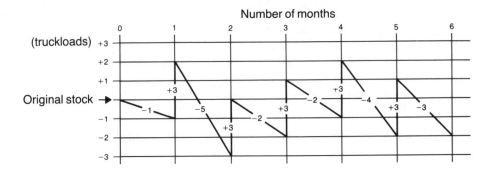

In this simulation, the minimum stock level is 3 truckloads below the original stock. So unless there were at least 3 truckloads in stock to start with, the warehouse would be unable to satisfy all its customers' demands during the period.

1   Carry out a few simulations of the process yourself.
    For each one, say what starting stock would be necessary if the warehouse is to satisfy all customers' demands during the period.

2   Suppose every month customers demand 6 truckloads. Work out the starting stock necessary to satisfy all demands.

The largest demand the warehouse would ever need to satisfy would be 6 truckloads in every one of the six months, and to satisfy all of these, a starting stock of 21 truckloads would be needed. However it is very unlikely that this maximum demand would occur. In fact the probability of this happening is $\left(\frac{1}{10}\right)^6 = 1$ in $1\,000\,000$.

Storing goods in a warehouse costs money, and it would be uneconomical to have 21 truckloads in stock just in case the maximum demand occurred. But starting with 21 (at least) is the only way to be absolutely certain that all demands will be satisfied. Starting with only 20 means that there is a tiny chance of not being able to satisfy all demands.

What the manager would like to know is the probability of being unable to satisfy all demands if he starts with 19, with 18, etc. Then he has to balance the cost of storing against the risk of being unable to satisfy demands, and the loss of money which that means.

To assess the risk of being unable to satisfy demands, the process can be simulated a large number of times. For each simulation we record how far the stock level fell below the starting value. We will call this the **deficit** for that particular simulation. (A listing for a computer program is printed in the teacher's guide.)

This table summarises the results of 4000 simulations on a computer. (In none of the simulations was the deficit 17, 18, 19, 20 or 21.)

Deficit	1	2	3	4	5	6	7	8
Frequency	102	227	460	532	609	588	454	346
Deficit	9	10	11	12	13	14	15	16
Frequency	271	180	104	68	26	15	15	3

Suppose the manager thinks of starting with a stock level of 13. Out of the 4000 simulations, there are 33 in which the deficit is more than 13. (We add together those whose deficits are 14, 15, and 16.)

So we estimate the probability of failing to satisfy all demands with a starting stock of 13 as being $\frac{33}{4000} = 0.00825$.

C3 Use the table above to estimate the probability of failing to satisfy all demands when the starting stock level is   (a) 10   (b) 5

Simulating a queue

Imagine a customs checkpoint on a road. Cars arrive, are checked, and are allowed to drive on. Only one car can be checked at a time. Sometimes a queue develops as cars wait at the checkpoint for their turn to be checked.

If cars arrive at a rapid rate, for example one every 10 seconds, but each one takes 60 seconds to be checked, then a queue of waiting cars will build up. If the interval between arrivals is large, say 5 minutes, but the checking time is only 1 minute, then there will be no hold-ups.

In practice, cars would arrive at irregular intervals, and checking times would vary from car to car. If we make some assumptions about how the intervals vary and how the checking times vary, then we can simulate what happens at the checkpoint.

We may want to know:

(a) What happens to the number of cars at the checkpoint (either being checked or waiting)? Does a long queue develop?

(b) For how long is the checkpoint idle (with no car being checked)?

(c) What is the average time spent by a car at the checkpoint?

There are three possible cases we can consider:

(1) Cars arrive at irregular intervals, but the checking time is the same for every car.

(2) Cars arrive at regular intervals, but the checking time varies.

(3) Cars arrive at irregular intervals, and the checking time varies.

(The fourth case, where both arrivals and checking times are regular is easy to deal with and does not need any simulation.)

Although case (2) is unrealistic when we are thinking about cars arriving at a checkpoint, it could apply to items coming off a factory assembly line or machine, for example, and being checked one by one.

To illustrate the simulation, we shall consider case (1) – irregular arrivals but constant checking time – and make the following assumptions:

Suppose the interval between arrivals is equally likely to be 0, 1, 2, 3, 4, 5, 6, 7, 8 or 9 minutes.

Suppose the checking time is 5 minutes for every car.

We shall assume that the checkpoint is idle to start with, and we will start measuring time from the moment the first car arrives.

To get the intervals between the first and second arrival, the second and third, etc., we use an ordinary random number generator.

Suppose it gives the sequence: 3 4 9 2 2 0 1 7
This goes in the first column of the table below.

The second column is obtained from the first by adding each interval to the previous arrival time.

The column 'length of check' consists of all 5s.

Interval between arrivals	Arrival time	Time at which check starts	Length of check	Time at which check ends	Time spent at checkpoint
–	0		5		
3	3		5		
4	7		5		
9	16		5		
⋮	⋮		⋮		

When these three columns have been filled in, the rest of the table is filled in row by row.

The important thing to remember is that the time at which a check starts is **either** the time at which the previous check ends, **or** the arrival time, whichever is **later**. (A car's check cannot start before it arrives!)

The 'time spent at checkpoint' includes checking time and any waiting time, so it is the time between arriving and finally leaving the checkpoint.

Following these rules, the table on the opposite page can be filled in as shown below.

Interval between arrivals	Arrival time	Time at which check starts	Length of check	Time at which check ends	Time spent at checkpoint
	0	0	5	5	5
3	3	5	5	10	7
4	7	10	5	15	8
9	16	16	5	21	5
⋮	⋮	⋮	⋮	⋮	⋮

Make a blank table, with columns as above. Use a random number generator to generate a sequence of nine random numbers, and write them in the first column of your table. Fill in the second column, and the fourth column (all 5s). Complete your table.

Calculate the mean time spent at the checkpoint by the ten cars.

It is easy to modify the method to deal with a case in which both arrivals and checking times are irregular.

Suppose we assume that intervals between arrivals behave as before, and that the checking time also is equally likely to be 0, 1, 2, ... , 9.

Instead of filling in the fourth column with all 5s, we generate a second random sequence for this column. After that we continue to complete the table as before.

Generate a sequence of nine random numbers for intervals between arrivals, and another sequence of ten random numbers for checking times.

Make a table as before.

Calculate the mean time spent at the checkpoint by the ten cars.

In the simulation below, both arrival intervals and checking times are equally likely to be 0, 1, 2, . . ., 9. The simulation was continued to cover a period of 60 minutes.

Interval between arrivals	Arrival time	Time at which check starts	Length of check	Time at which check ends	Time spent at checkpoint
–	0	0	9	9	9
1	1	9	1	10	9
2	3	10	7	17	14
1	4	17	3	20	16
3	7	20	6	26	19
3	10	26	0	26	16
8	18	26	8	34	16
5	23	34	0	34	11
6	29	34	6	40	11
8	37	40	1	41	4
8	45	45	8	53	8
2	47	53	1	54	7
0	47	54	4	58	11
2	49	58	8	(66)	17
8	51	(66)	1	(67)	10

We can draw a graph showing the number of cars at the checkpoint. We first use the 2nd and 5th columns to mark arrivals (▲) and departures (▼) below the time axis, and then use these marks as a guide to drawing the graph.

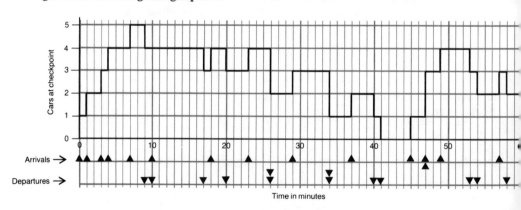

From the graph it is easy to see that the checkpoint was idle for 4 minutes out of 60.

It is also possible to calculate the mean number of cars at the checkpoint. We use the graph to find for how many minutes there were 0 cars, for how many there was 1 car, and so on.

Number of cars	Time in minutes
0	4
1	7
2	13
3	14
4	20
5	2
Total	60

The mean number of cars is

$$\frac{(0 \times 4) + (1 \times 7) + (2 \times 13) + (3 \times 14) + (4 \times 20) + (5 \times 2)}{60}$$

$$= 2 \cdot 75.$$

Of course we do not get much useful information from a single short simulation such as this. The mean number of cars waiting happened to be 2·75 in this particular trial of the simulation. But is that typical, unusually high, or unusually low?

To get more reliable information we need to run the simulation a large number of times, and once again a computer is the ideal tool.

A computer simulation of the checkpoint

There is a listing for the program described below in the teacher's guide.

In the example shown on the opposite page, the interval between arrivals can be 0, 1, 2, 3, 4, 5, 6, 7, 8 or 9 minutes with equal probabilities. The same is true for the checking times.

In the simulation program also, the interval between arrivals can be 0, 1, 2, . . ., 9 minutes but you can choose the probabilities yourself. The same is true of the checking times.

The program first asks you to assign a probability to each of the possible intervals between arrivals: 0, 1, 2, . . ., 9.

You input each probability as a percentage (whole numbers only). An example is shown on the right.

You are then asked to assign a probability to each of the possible checking times.

Interval between arrivals	Probability
0	0
1	0
2	20
3	30
4	40
5	10
6	0
7	0
8	0
9	0

The computer then simulates what happens at the checkpoint during a period of 100 minutes, starting from the arrival of the first car. It will produce a graph similar to the one on page 102.

It will also give you the following information about that particular trial:

The maximum number of cars at the checkpoint.

The mean number of cars at the checkpoint.

The mean time spent by a car at the checkpoint.
(Cars which arrived but did not leave the checkpoint during the 100 minutes are not included in this calculation.)

The percentage of the time for which the checkpoint was idle.

So far you will have done one trial only. You will not know whether the four values you get for the maximum number of cars, etc., are typical or unusual (given the probabilities you started with).

So, without changing the probabilities, you run the simulation several times. Each time the computer will calculate the four quantities listed above.

You can ask the computer to produce a table showing, for each trial, the values of the four quantitites. By examining this table, you can get an idea of how much variation there is among the trials.

Then you can change the probabilities and carry out the whole procedure again.

2 The Fibonacci sequence

The mathematician Leonardo of Pisa, also known as Fibonacci, was born at Pisa in Italy in 1175. He was largely responsible for spreading the use of Arabic numerals (0, 1, 2, 3, . . .) throughout Europe. Previously, calculations had been done by complicated methods using Roman numerals.

Leonardo investigated a number of mathematical problems. One of these gives rise to the sequence which bears his name – the Fibonacci sequence.

The original problem was about rabbits.

> Someone put a pair of rabbits in a certain place, surrounded on all sides by a wall, to find out how many pairs of rabbits will be born there during one year. It is assumed that every month a pair of rabbits produces another pair, and that rabbits begin to bear young two months after their birth.

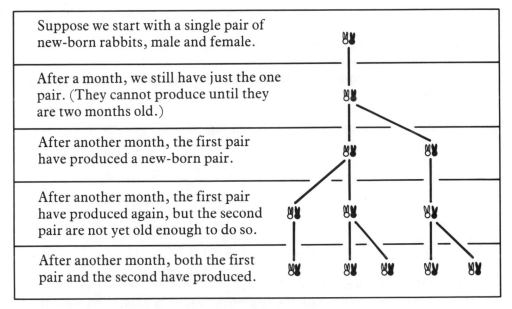

Continue the diagram for the next three months.
Look at the number of pairs after 1 month, 2 months, etc.
Can you see a pattern in the way the numbers build up?

The number of pairs of rabbits increases like this:

    1   1   2   3   5   8   13   21   34

Each number is the sum of the previous two numbers.

We can state this rule in the notation used for sequences.
Let f (for Fibonacci) stand for the sequence above. Here is a table of values of f.

f_1	f_2	f_3	f_4	f_5	f_6	f_7	f_8	f_9	...
1	1	2	3	5	8	13	21	34	...

If, for example, we add f_4 and f_5, we get the value of f_6.

The general rule is $f_n + f_{n+1} = f_{n+2}$.

This rule can be used to generate the whole sequence, provided we know the values of f_1 and f_2 to start with. We shall always assume that $f_1 = 1$ and $f_2 = 1$.

2 Continue the Fibonacci sequence as far as f_{15}.

3 Explain why the numbers in the sequence go 'odd, odd, even; odd, odd, even; . . .'.

4 If we add up the terms as we go through the sequence, we get this:

f_1 $= 1$ $= 1$

$f_1 + f_2$ $= 1 + 1$ $= 2$

$f_1 + f_2 + f_3$ $= 1 + 1 + 2$ $= 4$

$f_1 + f_2 + f_3 + f_4$ $= 1 + 1 + 2 + 3$ $= 7$

$f_1 + f_2 + f_3 + f_4 + f_5$ $= 1 + 1 + 2 + 3 + 5 = 12$

Look at the sequence of totals: 1, 2, 4, 7, 12. Continue it for a few more terms. Compare it with the sequence f itself. What do you notice?

The sequence of totals goes 1, 2, 4, 7, 12, 20, 33, . . .
Each term here is 1 less than a term of the sequence f.
We can see this most clearly by writing the totals below the sequence f.

f_1	f_2	f_3	f_4	f_5	f_6	f_7	f_8	f_9	f_{10}	. . .
1	1	2	3	5	8	13	21	34	55	. . .
1	1	4	7	12	20	33	54	88	143	. . .

This is the value of $f_1 + f_2 + f_3 + f_4 + f_5$. And it is equal to $f_7 - 1$.

The general rule appears to be $f_1 + f_2 + f_3 + \ldots + f_n = f_{n+2} - 1$.

We can prove that this rule is true. The proof is given here to illustrate how facts about the Fibonacci sequence can be proved by algebra. We start from the basic facts about the sequence, which are that $f_n + f_{n+1} = f_{n+2}$ and that $f_1 = 1$ and $f_2 = 1$.

The equation $f_n + f_{n+1} = f_{n+2}$ can be written in other equivalent forms, which are also useful:

$$f_n = f_{n+2} - f_{n+1} \qquad f_{n+1} = f_{n+2} - f_n$$

In the proof here we make use of the form $f_n = f_{n+2} - f_{n+1}$.

$$\text{We know that } f_1 = f_3 - f_2$$
$$f_2 = f_4 - f_3$$
$$f_3 = f_5 - f_4$$
$$f_4 = f_6 - f_5$$
$$\vdots$$
$$f_n = f_{n+2} - f_{n+1}$$

Now we add all these equations together. On the left-hand side we get $f_1 + f_2 + f_3 + \ldots + f_n$.

On the right-hand side most of the terms cancel out in pairs: f_3 in the top line cancels $-f_3$ in the second line, f_4 in the second line cancels $-f_4$ in the third line, etc.

The only terms which do not cancel out are $-f_2$ and f_{n+2}.

So $f_1 + f_2 + f_3 + \ldots + f_n = f_{n+2} - f_2 = \mathbf{f_{n+2} - 1}$ (because $f_2 = 1$)

5 Prove that $f_1 + f_3 + f_5 + f_7 + \ldots + f_{2n-1} = f_{2n}$.

   (**Hint.** The basic relation $f_n + f_{n+1} = f_{n+2}$ can be written $f_{n+1} = f_{n+2} - f_n$. Also, we know that $f_1 = f_2$. So we get these equations $f_1 = f_2$,
   $f_3 = f_4 - f_2$, etc.)

6 Prove that $f_2 + f_4 + f_6 + \ldots + f_{2n} = f_{2n+1} - 1$.

7 Prove that $f_1 - f_2 + f_3 - f_4 + f_5 - \ldots + f_{2n-1} - f_{2n} = {}^-f_{2n-1} + 1$

   Deduce that $f_1 - f_2 + f_3 - f_4 + \ldots - f_{2n} + f_{2n+1} = f_{2n} + 1$.

8 Show that $f_n f_{n+1} - f_{n-1} f_n = f_n^2$.

   Use this to write down expressions for $f_2^2, f_3^2, \ldots, f_n^2$ and deduce that

   $$f_2^2 + f_3^2 + \ldots + f_n^2 = f_n f_{n+1} - f_1 f_2$$

9 This diagram can be extended indefinitely, with the squares building up in a 'spiral' pattern.

   The sides of the squares are the Fibonacci numbers 1, 1, 2, 3, 5, 8, . . .

   Use the diagram to explain why

   $f_1^2 + f_2^2 + f_3^2 + f_4^2 + f_5^2 + f_6^2 = f_6 f_7$.

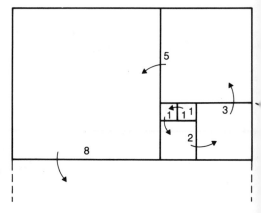

10 Take the pairs consisting of each Fibonacci number and the next one. Think of them as coordinates and plot them on squared paper.

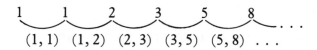

   What do you notice about the points as you get further and further along the sequence? Draw a 'line of best fit' through the origin and measure its gradient.

The ratios of successive terms of the Fibonacci sequence

1 Calculate the values of $\dfrac{f_2}{f_1}$, $\dfrac{f_3}{f_2}$, $\dfrac{f_4}{f_3}$, $\dfrac{f_5}{f_4}$, and so on up to $\dfrac{f_{10}}{f_9}$.

What appears to happen to the value $\dfrac{f_{n+1}}{f_n}$ as n increases?

If we go back to the basic relation $f_n + f_{n+1} = f_{n+2}$, and divide both sides by f_{n+1}, we get

$$\dfrac{f_n}{f_{n+1}} + 1 = \dfrac{f_{n+2}}{f_{n+1}} \qquad (1)$$

We will let r_n stand for the ratio $\dfrac{(n+1)\text{th term}}{n\text{th term}}$, or $\dfrac{f_{n+1}}{f_n}$.

So r_{n+1} will mean the ratio $\dfrac{(n+2)\text{th term}}{(n+1)\text{th term}} = \dfrac{f_{n+2}}{f_{n+1}}$.

We can re-state equation (1) using r_n and r_{n+1}:

$$\dfrac{1}{r_n} + 1 = r_{n+1} \qquad (2)$$

We can use this equation to generate the values of $r_1, r_2, r_3, r_4, \ldots$ without going back to the original Fibonacci numbers. All we need to know is that the first ratio, r_1, which is $\dfrac{f_2}{f_1}$, is equal to 1.

$r_1 = 1$

$r_2 = \dfrac{1}{r_1} + 1 = \dfrac{1}{1} + 1 = 2$

$r_3 = \dfrac{1}{r_2} + 1 = \dfrac{1}{2} + 1 = 1 \cdot 5$

$r_4 = \dfrac{1}{r_3} + 1 = \dfrac{1}{1 \cdot 5} + 1 = 1 \cdot 666 \ldots$

and so on.

2 Use the relation $r_{n+1} = \dfrac{1}{r_n} + 1$ to continue the calculation up to r_{10}.

The sequence $r_1, r_2, r_3, \ldots$ appears to converge towards a number in the region of 1·62.

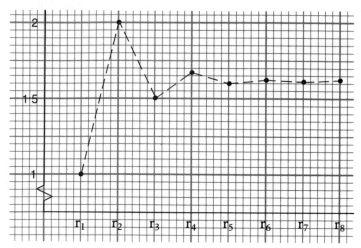

Let r be the limit which the sequence $r_1, r_2, r_3, \ldots$ converges towards.

As n gets larger, both r_n and the next term r_{n+1} become more nearly equal to r. So in the iteration formula, replace both r_n and r_{n+1} by r.

So $r_{n+1} = \dfrac{1}{r_n} + 1$ becomes $r = \dfrac{1}{r} + 1$.

(In other words, r is a **fixed point** of the iteration formula.)

13 Show that the equation $r = \dfrac{1}{r} + 1$ can be written as $r^2 - r - 1 = 0$.

Solve this equation by 'completing the square'. There are two solutions, one positive and one negative. Only the positive value of r is wanted here. Show that its exact value is $\dfrac{\sqrt{5} + 1}{2}$.

The number $r = \dfrac{\sqrt{5} + 1}{2}$ is often called the 'golden ratio'.

Here we have arrived at it by looking at the ratios of successive terms of the Fibonacci sequence, but the golden ratio also arises in other situations.

14 Many artists have thought that the most pleasing shape for a rectangular frame or window is one where

if you remove a square, like this, ...   the remaining rectangle is similar to the original one.

Show that for this to be true, the ratio $\dfrac{\text{height}}{\text{width}}$ of the rectangle must be equal to r, the golden ratio.

(The process of removing a square can be continued, giving an infinite sequence of *'golden rectangles'*.)

15 Show that in a regular pentagon the ratio $\dfrac{\text{diagonal}}{\text{side}}$ is equal to r.

Further problems on the Fibonacci sequence

16 A sequence u starts with the first two terms $u_1 = a$ and $u_2 = b$. But apart from that it behaves like the Fibonacci sequence, So $u_n + u_{n+1} = u_{n+2}$.

Write down expressions for $u_3, u_4, u_5, \ldots$, up to u_8, in terms of a and b. What do you notice? Write a formula for u_n in terms of a, b and terms of the Fibonacci sequence f.

17 A sequence v starts with the first two terms $v_1 = 1$ and $v_2 = r$, where r is the golden ratio. The sequence obeys the rule $v_n + v_{n+1} = v_{n+2}$.

Explain why the sequence v is a geometric sequence.

18 Draw the diagram on page 108 on squared paper. Mark the centres of the squares. What do you notice about the centres? Can you prove it?

13 Rational and irrational numbers

A Recurring decimals

To change a fraction to a decimal you divide the numerator (top number) by the denominator (bottom number).

For example, $\frac{7}{16}$ (= 7 ÷ 16) = 0·4375.

The result in this case 'comes out' **exactly** to 0·4375.

If you change $\frac{7}{11}$ to a decimal, you get 0·6363636363 . . .

The pair of figures '63' repeats, or **recurs**, again and again, for ever.

You can't tell this from a calculator (although you might guess that it is true). If you do 7 ÷ 11 on an ordinary 8-figure calculator, you get 0·6363636, which is only an approximation.

But if you do 7 ÷ 11 on paper, you can see **why** the pair 63 recurs.

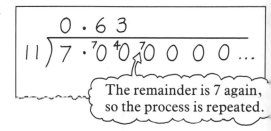

The remainder is 7 again, so the process is repeated.

In all the questions in this section, do the divisions **on paper**.

A1 Change each of these fractions to decimals.

(a) $\frac{1}{3}$ (b) $\frac{1}{9}$ (c) $\frac{1}{6}$ (d) $\frac{1}{7}$ (e) $\frac{1}{11}$

If a single figure recurs, we write a dot over it to show this.

0·444444 . . . is written 0·$\dot{4}$.   0·722222 . . . is written 0·7$\dot{2}$.

If a group of figures recurs, we write a dot over the first and last figures in the group.

0·434343 . . . is written 0·$\dot{4}\dot{3}$.   0·8195195195 . . . is written 0·8$\dot{1}$9$\dot{5}$.

Here is the calculation for $\frac{1}{7}$.

```
       0 · 1   4   2   8   5   7   1   4   2   8   5   7   1 ...
7 ) 1 · ¹0  ³0  ²0  ⁶0  ⁴0  ⁵0  ¹0  ³0  ²0  ⁶0  ⁴0  ⁵0  ¹0 ...
```

There are **two** recurring patterns in calculations of this kind.
One is the pattern of the decimal: 0·14285142857 . . .
The other is the pattern of the **remainders**, which goes

    1, 3, 2, 6, 4, 5, 1, 3, 2, 6, 4, 5, ...

A2 What is the pattern of   (i) the remainders

                           (ii) the figures in the recurring decimal

in the calculation for   (a) $\frac{2}{7}$ (b) $\frac{3}{7}$ (c) $\frac{4}{7}$ (d) $\frac{5}{7}$ (e) $\frac{6}{7}$

A3 Now you are going to find the recurring decimal for $\frac{1}{17}$.

Before doing $\frac{1}{17}$ on paper, it is useful to make a '17-times table'.

(You can use a calculator for this!)

```
17 ×    1    2    3    4    5    . . .
       17   34   51   68   85
```

The calculation for $\frac{1}{17}$ starts like this:

```
        0 · 0   5   8   8   2   3   ...
17 ) 1 · ¹0  ¹⁰0  ¹⁵0  ¹⁴0  ⁴0  ⁶0  ⁹0   0  ...
```

(a) Copy and complete the calculation until the figures start to recur.

(b) Even before doing the calculation it is possible to be certain that there cannot be more than 16 figures in the recurring group in the decimal. Why is this? (Think of the remainders.)

(c) Look at the sequence of remainders. Can you say what the decimal for $\frac{2}{17}$ will be, without doing any further calculations?

What about the decimal for $\frac{3}{17}$?

The complete calculation for $\frac{1}{17}$ is as follows.

$$\begin{array}{r}0.0\;5\;8\;8\;2\;3\;5\;2\;9\;4\;1\;1\;7\;6\;4\;7\ldots\\17\overline{)1.{}^{1}0\;{}^{10}0\;{}^{15}0\;{}^{14}0\;{}^{4}0\;{}^{6}0\;{}^{9}0\;{}^{5}0\;{}^{16}0\;{}^{7}0\;{}^{2}0\;{}^{3}0\;{}^{13}0\;{}^{11}0\;{}^{8}0\;{}^{12}0\;{}^{1}0}\end{array}$$

The remainders go

1, 10, 15, 14, 4, 6, 9, 5, 16, 7, 2, 3, 13, 11, 8, 12, then again . . .

This calculation goes through every possible remainder from 1 to 16, and this is why there are 16 recurring figures in the decimal. There cannot be more than 16, because there are only 16 different possible remainders.

When we calculate $\frac{2}{17}$, the first remainder is 2. So if we look at the calculation for $\frac{1}{17}$, we can see where the calculations for $\frac{2}{17}$ will start.

$$\begin{array}{r}0.1\;1\;7\;6\;4\;7\ldots\\17\overline{)2.{}^{2}0\;{}^{3}0\;{}^{13}0\;{}^{11}0\;{}^{8}0\;{}^{12}0\;{}^{1}0}\end{array}$$

In this diagram, the sequence of remainders is written round the inside of the circle, and the figures of the decimal round the outside.

The recurring figures in the decimals for $\frac{2}{17}$, $\frac{3}{17}$, etc. are found by starting at different places on the circle.

We say that the figures for $\frac{2}{17}$, $\frac{3}{17}$, etc. are each a **cyclical permutation** of the figures for $\frac{1}{17}$.

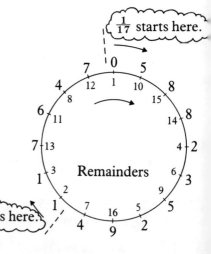

A4 Write down the recurring decimal for (a) $\frac{5}{17}$ (b) $\frac{15}{17}$

5 (a) What is the maximum possible number of recurring figures in the decimal for $\frac{1}{13}$?

(b) Work out the decimal for $\frac{1}{13}$. Does it have the maximum possible number of recurring figures?

(c) Why can't you use the calculation for $\frac{1}{13}$ to write down the decimal for $\frac{2}{13}$?

(d) Work out the decimal for $\frac{2}{13}$.
Can you write down the decimals for $\frac{3}{13}$, $\frac{4}{13}$, etc. up to $\frac{12}{13}$?
Which ones are cyclical permutations of $\frac{1}{13}$, and which of $\frac{2}{13}$?

B Using a calculator

So far we have not used a calculator, because it is limited to a certain number of figures. However, with a little ingenuity, we can use it to get recurring decimals even when there are long recurring groups of figures.

Here we assume that an 8-figure calculator is being used. (If your calculator has more figures, that makes the task easier.) It is important that the calculator **must not round up the last figure**.

Example Find the recurring decimal for $\frac{1}{19}$.

We use the fact that some of the decimals for $\frac{1}{19}$, $\frac{2}{19}$, $\frac{3}{19}$, etc., will be cyclical permutations of others.
We know that the maximum possible number of recurring figures is 18.

On the calculator, $\frac{1}{19} = 0 \cdot 0526315$. *(These suggest that $\frac{2}{19}$ continues with a 5.)*

$\frac{2}{19} = 0 \cdot 1052631$

$\frac{3}{19} = 0 \cdot 1578947$ *(Perhaps this is the '15' at the end of $\frac{1}{19}$. If so, we could 'extend' $\frac{1}{19}$ to $0 \cdot 052631578947$.)*

31 Continue this process, and find the complete recurring decimal for $\frac{1}{19}$.

32 Use a calculator to find the recurring decimal for (a) $\frac{1}{23}$ (b) $\frac{1}{29}$

C Terminating decimals

A decimal which 'stops' after so many places is called a **terminating** decimal.

C1 When you change these fractions to decimals, some will give terminating decimals and some will give recurring decimals. For each fraction, say whether the decimal terminates or recurs.

In each case, try to answer first without doing any calculation. Then check your answer by calculation. (You can use a calculator for checking.)

(a) $\frac{3}{5}$ (b) $\frac{3}{8}$ (c) $\frac{5}{12}$ (d) $\frac{8}{15}$ (e) $\frac{4}{25}$ (f) $\frac{13}{40}$ (g) $\frac{13}{60}$ (h) $\frac{6}{15}$

(i) $\frac{19}{125}$ (j) $\frac{19}{128}$ (k) $\frac{11}{70}$ (l) $\frac{5}{32}$ (m) $\frac{7}{32}$ (n) $\frac{27}{80}$ (o) $\frac{25}{72}$ (p) $\frac{14}{224}$

C2 How can you tell whether a fraction will give a terminating decimal or a recurring decimal?
Make sure that your 'rule' gives the right answer for each of the fractions listed in question C1.

D Changing decimals to fractions

Terminating decimals are easily changed to fractions.

For example, $0 \cdot 6 = \frac{6}{10} = \frac{3}{5}$

$$0 \cdot 63 = \frac{63}{100}$$

$$0 \cdot 648 = \frac{648}{1000} = \frac{324}{500} = \frac{162}{250} = \frac{81}{125}$$

D1 Change these decimals to fractions.

(a) $0 \cdot 85$ (b) $0 \cdot 408$ (c) $0 \cdot 0256$ (d) $0 \cdot 0125$

Recurring decimals can also be changed to fractions, but the method is ingenious.

Example Change $0.\dot{8}$ to a fraction.

> Let f be the fraction which is equivalent to $0.\dot{8}$.
>
> $f = 0.888888\ldots$
>
> If we multiply f by 10, each figure 8 moves one place to the left.
>
> $10f = 8.888\,888\ldots$
>
> Now we subtract the first equation from the second. The infinite string of 8s above one another will cancel out.
>
> $9f = 8.000\,000$
>
> Then we divide both sides by 9.
>
> $f = \dfrac{8}{9}$

D2 The method above works because when the first equation is subtracted from the second, the 8s above one another cancel out.

Adapt the method to change each of these to a fraction.

(a) $0.4\dot{3}$ (b) $0.4\dot{7}$ (c) $0.\dot{4}\dot{7}$ (d) $0.\dot{3}8\dot{4}$ (e) $0.7\dot{2}\dot{1}$

D3 (a) Use the method to change $0.\dot{9}$ to a fraction. Is the result correct?

(b) It is easy to show that $\frac{1}{9} = 0.111111\ldots$.

So it follows that $\frac{9}{9} = 0.9999999\ldots$

Does this convince you that $0.\dot{9} = 1$?

> But $0.9999\ldots$ means start with $\frac{9}{10}$, add on $\frac{9}{100}$, then $\frac{9}{1000}$, and so on! No matter how far you go, you will still not reach 1.

> But suppose you go on **FOR EVER**?

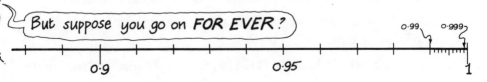

E Irrational numbers

So far we have looked at two kinds of decimal: terminating and recurring. We have seen that

(1) every fraction is equivalent to either a terminating decimal or a recurring decimal (for example, $\frac{23}{59}$ must recur after at most 58 figures);

(2) every terminating or recurring decimal can be changed to an equivalent fraction.

We usually think of fractions as being less than 1, but it is useful to have 'fractions' like $\frac{7}{4}$ which are greater than 1.

We use the term **rational number** to include all numbers of the form $\frac{a}{b}$, where a and b are whole numbers. So $\frac{2}{3}$, $\frac{7}{4}$, $\frac{9137}{5069}$, $43 \left(= \frac{43}{1}\right)$ are all examples of rational numbers.

We can re-state the two facts above in terms of rational numbers. The decimal form of a number is often called its **decimal expansion**, so the two facts (1) and (2) are as follows.

> (1) The decimal expansion of every rational number either terminates or recurs.
>
> (2) Every terminating or recurring decimal expansion is the expansion of a rational number.

We have not yet considered decimal expansions which neither terminate nor recur. Here is one example of an infinite decimal which does **not** recur:

0·12112111211112111112 . . .

This one happens to have a pattern to it, but is **not** a recurring decimal. So there is **no** rational number, of the form $\frac{a}{b}$, which is equivalent to it.

The number 0·12112111211112111112 . . . is called an **irrational** number.

Irrational numbers arise frequently in mathematics. An important example is $\sqrt{2}$. Later we will prove that $\sqrt{2}$ must be an irrational number.

If we try to calculate $\sqrt{2}$ by the decimal search method, we find that

        1·4 is too small.   1·5 is too big.
        1·14 is too small.   1·42 is too big.
        1·414 is too small.   1·415 is too big.

              and so on.

If we go to eight decimal places, we find that $\sqrt{2}$ is somewhere between

       1·41421356 and 1·41421357.

So far the decimal expansion of $\sqrt{2}$ shows no pattern. But we could never be sure simply by working out more and more decimal places. Even if we worked it out to 1 000 000 decimal places, then it might still terminate or start to recur after the 1 000 001th place!

However, it is not difficult to prove that it **cannot terminate**. Question E1 shows how to prove this.

Suppose the decimal expansion of $\sqrt{2}$ terminates, and the last figure is 1. In other words, suppose that $\sqrt{2} = 1·\ldots\ldots\ldots\ldots\ldots 1$.

If you multiply this supposed value for $\sqrt{2}$ by itself, what will the last figure of the result be?
This proves that the decimal expansion of $\sqrt{2}$ cannot end in a 1.

Prove that it cannot end in any other figure.

The method of proof in question E1 is called 'indirect' proof.

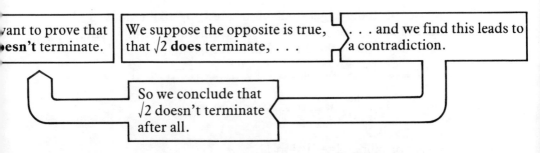

So far we have proved that the decimal expansion of $\sqrt{2}$ does not terminate. But we haven't proved that it doesn't recur, so it is still possible that $\sqrt{2}$ may be equal to a rational number.

In other words, we may be able to find two whole numbers a and b such that $\dfrac{a}{b}$ is equal to $\sqrt{2}$.

One way to search for such a rational number is to use a table of squares.

The table below gives the squares of whole numbers from 0 to 99. To find the square of 56, for example, you go to row 50 and column 6, and find $56^2 = 3136$.

	0	1	2	3	4	5	6	7	8	9
0	0	1	4	9	16	25	36	49	64	81
10	100	121	144	169	196	225	256	289	324	361
20	400	441	484	529	576	625	676	729	784	841
30	900	961	1024	1089	1156	1225	1296	1369	1444	1521
40	1600	1681	1764	1849	1936	2025	2116	2209	2304	2401
50	2500	2601	2704	2809	2916	3025	3136	3249	3364	3481
60	3600	3721	3844	3969	4096	4225	4356	4489	4624	4761
70	4900	5041	5184	5329	5476	5625	5776	5929	6084	6241
80	6400	6561	6724	6889	7056	7225	7396	7569	7744	7921
90	8100	8281	8464	8649	8836	9025	9216	9409	9604	9801

We can use this table to get some quite good approximations to $\sqrt{2}$. The method is this: look for two square numbers, one of which is approximately 2 times the other. For example,

7386 (which is 86^2) is approximately 2 times **3721** (which is 61^2).

So it follows that $\dfrac{86^2}{61^2}$ is approximately equal to 2.

So $\dfrac{86}{61}$ is approximately equal to $\sqrt{2}$.

Use the table to find some more approximations to $\sqrt{2}$, of the form $\frac{a}{b}$.

Suppose you have **no idea** of the decimal expansion of $\sqrt{2}$, even to a few decimal places, and no $\sqrt{}$ key on your calculator.

How could you verify that $\frac{41}{29}$ is quite a good approximation to $\sqrt{2}$?

Without using the $\sqrt{}$ key or any knowledge about the value of $\sqrt{2}$, use a calculator to find out which of these is the best approximation to $\sqrt{2}$.

$$\frac{762}{539} \qquad \frac{222}{157} \qquad \frac{541}{383} \qquad \frac{181}{128}$$

The table of squares can be used in a similar way to get approximations to $\sqrt{3}$.

Use the table to find some approximations to $\sqrt{3}$.

Use the table to find some approximations to (a) $\sqrt{5}$ (b) $\sqrt{10}$

Nowhere in the table is there a square number which is exactly 2 times another square number.

That is why we cannot use the table to find a rational number $\frac{a}{b}$

which is **exactly** equal to $\sqrt{2}$.

But perhaps if the table were bigger, with square numbers up to 1000^2 or even 1000000^2, we might find an a^2 which is **exactly** 2 times a b^2, and then $\frac{a}{b}$ would be equal to $\sqrt{2}$.

In fact, the search for a rational number $\frac{a}{b}$ which is equal to $\sqrt{2}$

is a fruitless one, because it can be **proved** that there is **no** rational number whose square is 2.

The proof, on the next page, is another example of indirect proof. We start by supposing that there is a rational number whose square is 2, and we find that this leads to a contradiction.

A proof that √2 is irrational

Suppose $\frac{a}{b}$ is a rational number whose square is 2.

a and b might each be either odd or even, so there are four possibilities for $\frac{a}{b}$.

$$\frac{a}{b} = \frac{\text{odd}}{\text{odd}} \quad \text{or} \quad \frac{\text{odd}}{\text{even}} \quad \text{or} \quad \frac{\text{even}}{\text{odd}} \quad \text{or} \quad \frac{\text{even}}{\text{even}}.$$

In the case $\frac{a}{b} = \frac{\text{even}}{\text{even}}$, we can simplify by dividing top and bottom by 2. If the result is still $\frac{\text{even}}{\text{even}}$, we can continue to simplify until it is reduced to one of the other three cases.

So we have three possibilities to consider for $\frac{a}{b}$: $\frac{\text{odd}}{\text{odd}}$, $\frac{\text{odd}}{\text{even}}$, $\frac{\text{even}}{\text{odd}}$.

(1) Suppose $\frac{a}{b} = \frac{\text{odd}}{\text{odd}}$.

Then $\left(\frac{a}{b}\right)^2 = \frac{\text{odd} \times \text{odd}}{\text{odd} \times \text{odd}} = \frac{\text{odd}}{\text{odd}}$.

But $\frac{\text{odd}}{\text{odd}}$ cannot possibly be 2. (See the foot of the page if in doubt.)

(2) Suppose $\frac{a}{b} = \frac{\text{odd}}{\text{even}}$.

Then $\left(\frac{a}{b}\right)^2 = \frac{\text{odd} \times \text{odd}}{\text{even} \times \text{even}} = \frac{\text{odd}}{\text{even}}$.

But $\frac{\text{odd}}{\text{even}}$ cannot possibly be 2. (See the foot of the page if in doubt.)

If $\frac{\text{top number}}{\text{bottom number}} = 2$, then the top number is twice the bottom number.

This means that the top number would have to be **even**.

(3) Suppose $\dfrac{a}{b} = \dfrac{\text{even}}{\text{odd}}$

Then $\left(\dfrac{a}{b}\right)^2 = \dfrac{\text{even} \times \text{even}}{\text{odd} \times \text{odd}} = \dfrac{\text{even}}{\text{odd}}$, which could be equal to 2.

But when you multiply an even number by another even number, the result is divisible by 4.

So if $\dfrac{a}{b} = \dfrac{\text{even}}{\text{odd}}$, then $\left(\dfrac{a}{b}\right)^2 = \dfrac{\text{a number divisible by 4}}{\text{an odd number}}$.

But if $\dfrac{\text{a number divisible by 4}}{\text{an odd number}} = 2$,

it would follow that there is a number divisible by 4 which is 2 times an odd number. And this is impossible.

In all cases we have shown that $\left(\dfrac{a}{b}\right)^2$ cannot possibly be 2.

So $\sqrt{2}$ cannot be a rational number.
It follows that its decimal expansion does not recur.

Mathematicians in ancient Greece knew that $\sqrt{2}$ could not be a rational number. They became interested in $\sqrt{2}$ when it arose in geometry: a square whose sides are 1 unit has a diagonal of length $\sqrt{2}$ units.

This fact is a consequence of Pythagoras' theorem, but it can also be seen from the diagram shown below.

The unit square is split into two triangles T.

The dotted square consists of four of the triangles.
So the area of the dotted square is 2 square units.

So the sides of the dotted square are $\sqrt{2}$ units long.

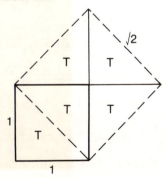

The fact that $\sqrt{2}$ is not equal to any rational number leads to some interesting consequences, which are explored in the next questions.

E7 The sloping line in this diagram has a gradient of $\sqrt{2}$.

Prove that no matter how far it is extended, it will never go through an intersection of two grid lines.

(Use the 'indirect' method of proof: suppose the line **does** go through an intersection (p, q).)

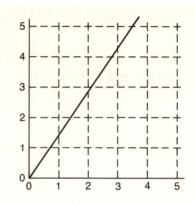

E8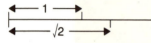

The points along the top of this line are marked off at intervals of 1 unit. The points along the bottom are marked off at intervals of $\sqrt{2}$ units.

At the start of the line, a top mark and a bottom mark coincide. Prove that this never happens again, no matter how far along the line you go.

E9 Two tiny insects move at the same speed. One walks round and round the perimeter of a square; the other walks backwards and forwards across a diagonal. They start together at one corner of the square. Prove that their positions never coincide again.

Summary

We have subdivided numbers into rational and irrational numbers.

Rational numbers can be written in the form $\frac{a}{b}$ where a and b are whole numbers. They have either terminating or recurring decimal expansions.

Irrational numbers cannot be written in the form $\frac{a}{b}$. Their decimal expansions are infinite but non-recurring. (Examples are $\sqrt{2}, \sqrt{3}, \pi$.)

The general name for rational and irrational numbers is **real numbers**.